10/14

D0662095

the house where

EVIL LURKS

About the Author

Brandon Callahan has been actively investigating paranormal activity in the field for over six years. He has worked on many private home investigations with varying levels of success. Callahan has also developed a method of tracking potential "hot spot" locations throughout the world that would be more likely to be prone to an abundance of paranormal activity. This method is still being refined, but it has been successful in almost every instance it has been implemented.

To Write the Author

If you wish to contact the author or would like more information about this book, please write to the author in care of Llewellyn Worldwide, and we will forward your request. Both the author and publisher appreciate hearing from you and learning of your enjoyment of this book and how it has helped you. Llewellyn Worldwide cannot guarantee that every letter written to the author can be answered, but all will be forwarded. Please write to:

Brandon Callahan
⁒ Llewellyn Worldwide
2143 Wooddale Drive
Woodbury, MN 55125-2989

Please enclose a self-addressed stamped envelope for reply,
or $1.00 to cover costs. If outside the USA, enclose
an international postal reply coupon.

A PARANORMAL INVESTIGATOR'S
MOST FRIGHTENING ENCOUNTER

the house where
EVIL LURKS

....

BRANDON CALLAHAN

Llewellyn Publications
Woodbury, Minnesota

FIRST EDITION
First Printing, 2014

Book design by Bob Gaul
Cover design by Kevin R. Brown
Cover image: iStockphoto.com/12566792/©WoodyUpstate
Editing by Ed Day

Llewellyn Publications is a registered trademark of Llewellyn Worldwide Ltd.

Library of Congress Cataloging-in-Publication Data
Callahan, Brandon.
  The house where evil lurks: a paranormal investigator's most
frightening encounter/Brandon Callahan.—First Edition.
    pages cm
  ISBN 978-0-7387-4066-9
1. Ghosts—Missouri. 2. Demonology—Missouri. 3. Occultism—Missouri.
4. Parapsychology—Missouri. I. Title.
  BF1472.U6C3525 2014
  133.1'29778—dc23

                    2014004787

Llewellyn Publications
A Division of Llewellyn Worldwide Ltd.
2143 Wooddale Drive
Woodbury, MN 55125-2989
www.llewellyn.com

Printed in the United States of America

Contents

Acknowledgments

To my endlessly supporting family: my wife, Nicole, and Bailey, Zachary, Evan, and Charlotte. You all inspire me on a daily basis and remind me that life is all about the loving adventures we all share every single day, and the wonderment of what may come tomorrow. To my mother, Bridget, and father, James, thank you for always putting yourselves behind the needs and desires of your family. You are the most selfless people I have ever known and we could not dream of having more perfect parents. My Aunt Janice, you have always inspired me to listen to my heart and soul and allow myself to think freely and follow my dreams. Thank you.

For those loved ones that have passed away over the years, Michael and Gabriel Rieke, R.J. Rhoades, and especially my grandparents, Joseph R. and Alice Callahan, you are the guardian angels that allow us all to go through life and enjoy the love and memories that have been provided over the generations. We can only hope to carry on with love in our hearts and you by our side.

To all of my friends, family, and supporters, thank you from the bottom of my heart. Never stop dreaming—the word *impossible* holds no meaning when you find yourself truly living your life. Follow your heart and dreams and never allow anybody to tell you "You can't." You truly can.

Introduction

I cannot allow myself to be deterred in my quest for enlightenment and the ability to help those souls in need, both the living and the dead. I do what I do not for accolades or gratitude, and certainly not for fame. I simply do what I feel I have been called to do. There are energies much greater than man at work in the world—there is Darkness and Light. I wander through the darkness to face my foe in hopes of helping just one person sleep better at night or to help one lost soul find their elusive eternal peace. The world is so much more than our everyday lives allow us to see. If you look, you may be surprised by what you find. I was.

I have always been drawn to anything that involves the unexplained. I have always sought the truth when it comes to what is real and what is not. About eight years ago, I decided to put together a group of like-minded people who wanted to go out and determine what is truly fact and what is fiction. I have always believed that all stories, as far-fetched as they may seem, are at least loosely based on facts. This is what drives me to go out into the world and do everything I can to find out the truth.

Over the years, I have found myself confronted with many things I once thought to be impossible. When I set out to find the mysteries of the world, I quickly came face to face with things that forced me to re-evaluate my beliefs, my faith, and what I truly understood. Fortunately, I was blessed by being surrounded by incredible people with different skill sets, which would allow us to do amazing work under any circumstances.

From the very beginning, I wanted to do this, but I wanted to do it right. I reminded myself and those I worked with to focus on the big picture and never be side-tracked by instant gratification. We would focus on helping normal people who live in abnormal circumstances. We would do whatever we had to do to help them sleep in their homes with a level of comfort that all too often had been forgotten. Secondarily, I wanted to focus on developing theories that would advance the field of paranormal research. Rather than simply convincing people that these things exist, our goal would be to compile a significant body of evidence and develop theories that would allow us to anticipate where we *should* look for paranormal activity. I believe with all my heart that if we think these things are real, it would be a shame to focus our efforts on only "famous haunted" locations. That seems shortsighted to me. My question was "how can we develop a method to know where to find what we are looking for without having to rely on stories that are already told?" I have spent countless hours searching for the answer to that question.

The following is the true story of a case my team and I spent four months working on. When we took on this case, we had worked together as a team for three years on several cases and conducted dozens of investigations, including several at private homes, like this one. Most recently, we successfully helped a man resolve what had become a violent and oppressive situation.

Going into the case with Shane and his family, I was very confident that no matter what we came into contact with, we would be able to find a resolution for them because we had successfully helped others rid their homes of negative energy. As it turned out, I had no idea what we were walking into, and we were unprepared for so many things to happen in such a short period of time. It was not long before we were all affected by the dark force that had taken over Shane's house. We have all seen movies and read stories about the evil that inhabits the world; until you are face to face with true fear and evil, there is no way to know how you will react. This is not a Hollywood story; this is a true story about one of the most frightening and dangerous homes I have ever stepped foot in.

One

THE BEGINNING

My soul will bear these scars for eternity.

I grew up in Kansas City, Missouri, and was blessed with a great family with sound values and was fortunate enough to receive a great education. From my earliest memories, I knew I had always been drawn toward anything that might be considered mysterious. I enjoyed playing in the basement during a stormy summer day re-enacting stories of ghosts and monsters. Something about the unknown always drew me in. I never felt like it was abnormal; I simply knew I had a very active imagination and never allowed myself to withdraw from something just because it seemed a little odd.

I grew up having dreams I remember. In one, I woke up in hysterics and remember my mom coming to my room and sitting on the side of my bed to calm me down. This was the first horrific dream that I can still remember like it happened yesterday. I believe I was ten years old. At the time, I was inconsolable. I had seen something in my dreams that had affected me in a deep and personal way, and I had no idea why. It was not a gory dream, nobody had died, and I was not trapped in a frightening situation. I could not understand why I was so scared, but I could not shake the feeling.

In the dream, we were driving as a family on a desert highway and I felt oddly both out of place and at home all at the same time. I could not put my finger on what was going on. There was very little discussion in the vehicle, and I could not focus on anything but the song on the radio. At the time I had the dream, I honestly don't believe I had ever even heard the song before in my life. I heard this song several years later in passing, and this dream and all those feelings washed over me like a tidal wave.

As I sit here now, I can hear the music and the words of Jim Morrison as the Doors play "Riders on the Storm." I had never heard this song to my recollection, but the song was clear as day in this dream. As it turned out, my mother was a very big fan of the Doors and they have since become a huge musical influence. The poetry and dark genius of Jim Morrison has resonated within me for most of my life. This particular night was my introduction to a man I would come to know as one of the greatest American artists ever born.

The haunting tune rang clear as my family made its way down the desert highway, and suddenly my focus was not on the stereotypical animal bones rotting in the desert sand underneath the searing sunshine, but on a distant plateau that seemed to stand hundreds of feet tall. There was nothing else in the distance as far as my eyes could reach besides this plateau, and it required my undivided attention.

Atop the plateau was a man. A man I have since seen to my personal horror, countless times throughout my life. Another man, whom I have difficulty speaking of, accompanied the man I know only as the Nemesis. He rarely says anything to me, but he is always there, there in my nightmares.

My nightmares are quite vivid and have become more commonplace over the last many years of my adult life, possibly from serving in the military. I have come to dread the thought of going to sleep on certain nights. It is as though I can anticipate the presence of the Nemesis and I always know when he wants to taunt me. I feel like I cannot escape his presence: The skeletal look to his face, always accompanied by a condescending and devious smile. His rotten teeth, stringy gray hair that flows randomly from the cover of his distinctly ratty black hat. His all-black attire is never far from my consciousness. He is always there. Though he spends most of his time in the dark corners of my mind, there are occasions when he makes his way to the forefront.

This night was my introduction to several things that would affect my life forever. This man, who to this day is too cowardly to declare a name, is always with me. He is more brazen when I am involved in disturbing situations and when my stress level is high. The environment we were in on that night when I was ten was symbolic in my future life as well. His eventual counterpart in my nightmares would be established during a period of time I had spent in a place many would know as a land God had forgotten. The desert surroundings were always eerie to me, and when the Nemesis's sidekick was given reason to show up permanently in my nightmares, my life would be changed.

The Nemesis began to show up more frequently in the nights following my decision at age twenty-seven to pursue what I believe to be my calling in life. The sporadic visits turned into a nightly, almost constant presence at times while I was investigating. I put myself in dangerous and disturbing situations voluntarily so I can do my best to help people in need. I ask for no accolades, I simply give you reason to know why I made some difficult decisions to do what I do. I cannot count how many times I have seen that eerie, condescending smile that stretches from ear to ear underneath those hollow eyes with the blackness that circles their sunken existence.

As I grew older, I was faced with many questions regarding my spirituality and what I truly believed. I was raised in a Catholic family and have always felt in touch with many of the Church's teachings. However, I was unaware of a stigma attached to Catholicism until I really made my way out into the world. It was always normal to me, and I had to come to grips with the fact that it was actually very different from the teaching of many other religions. I cannot say that I ever felt judged or persecuted, but it was made very clear that a lot of people look at Catholicism as something of a mystery. I have always accepted the differences of others and felt this was just something I would have to understand.

During my days as a young adult, the Catholic Church came under fire because of all the scandals that were made public, and I immediately felt lied to and cheated. I quickly developed a personal issue with the Church and distanced myself from what I had been taught for the first eighteen years of my life. As I sat in the middle of yet another war being waged overseas, I could see one organized religion after another involve themselves in public hatred pointed at people who pray differently than they do. At one point, as I was surrounded by hatred and death, I convinced myself that organized religion was nothing but another word for corruption and an excuse to hate people because of their differences. This was heartbreaking because I had to realize I was simply too naive as a young adult to grasp the fact that the world was full of danger and groups of people finding reasons to hate others.

As my days in the Air Force came to an end in 2003, and I was heading back to the States from my extended stay overseas, I felt like I would bring many life lessons back with me. My hope was that those experiences would help me find myself, as I knew I was a very different person than who I was when I left. While I was out receiving my life education, I had several encounters with people and situations that had again piqued my interest in the paranormal, and I began thinking about ways I could legitimately pursue answers to those questions. I felt in my heart that I had not lost "God," I had simply lost the ability to be manipulated by the teachings of man. I needed to find out what I truly believed and develop my own mind so I could be happier and more content with the world.

Within a couple years of getting back home, I had become more determined than ever to pursue the unexplainable. I knew I would have to be surrounded by the right people to go about this the right way. As I began to gather equipment, I knew who the core members should be as I started organizing a team that would make a difference in the world of paranormal research.

My brother Courtney and his wife, Jennifer, had come home from their own extended stay overseas where they met while being members of the U.S. Army. My brother "Snort," as he will be known throughout this story, had been medically discharged from the Army after falling off a cliff while on a night patrol near the DMZ in South Korea. Snort was a name that had developed over many years of abuse my younger brother endured at the hands of myself and our older brother. After his fall, he had to deal with endless trips to the doctor as he had developed awful pain in his back that had left him nearly crippled on more than one occasion. Approaching them with my idea was not a difficult proposition. Turned out, he and Jenn had experienced many paranormal events throughout their lives, so as I mentioned that I wanted to put together a team of investigators, they both quickly jumped on board. Snort had told me about a very frightening experience they had while living in a house in Kentucky. He said that he had been held down in bed by something he could not see, and they had all kinds of different experiences that had made them wonder what was inhabiting the house. They both also told me about some strange things going on in the house they were currently living in.

After Snort and Jenn told me about the disembodied voices they had been hearing throughout their house, and that their small kids had reported strange things as well, we felt like their home would be the perfect place to conduct our first investigation.

My brother and I had set a date for our investigation, so now I had to approach my very good friend R.J. about what we were going to do. R.J. and I always had a great time cooking up crazy ideas and plans together. R.J. was a very large man, but his red hair and freckle-covered face did not allow anyone to walk away without a smile when they interacted with him. And while it's become cliche to say someone is "just a big teddy bear," this description fits R.J. perfectly. His infectious smile and constant joking ways made him one of the most enjoyable people that I have ever come in contact with.

I knew R.J. would jump all over the idea I had cooked up. He and I were famous for coming up with outrageous ideas and plans to basically take over the world. His intelligence was unmatched and he had a genuine passion for life and experiencing anything life had to offer.

"Dude, we are doing this! I've told you about the weird shit that happened when I was in Turkey and I have a plan to go and check this shit out. I need to know what is real and what isn't."

"Hell yes! This is awesome!" R.J. replied in the way only he could.

From that second on, I knew he and I would find locations to conduct investigations at and eventually find what we were looking for. He and I both had a background in different types of technology and he was an absolute computer wizard. Going out to frightening locations and looking for things that go bump in the night was a no-brainer. I knew if I led, he would follow. This is how I knew things would shake out; he would make himself available and be an invaluable part of the team, but I would have to take the initiative and really research how to go about putting this together.

The team came together quickly and involved some incredible people, but I knew I was missing something. I had done years of research on just about everything involving the paranormal, but I had no field experience whatsoever.

I happened to have just started a new job with a friend of mine I had worked with for several years and we always clicked. I decided to speak to Jason Buis at work about what I was trying to do. Something had told me that Jason could help me, and sure enough, we sat down and spoke for hours about his history in and passion for this field of research. Jason grew up dealing with the paranormal all his life because he is a very sensitive medium, though he noted that he had got out of the field years ago because he'd had some disturbing encounters, not only with spirits, but with people who were in the field for all the wrong reasons. We talked about how dangerous this field of research was and how important it was to do this for the right reasons and be surrounded by the right people. I let Jason know about the investigation we were about to conduct at my brother's house, and he allowed me to borrow one of his recorders and wished us luck.

It was Valentine's Day weekend, but I remember that investigation like it was yesterday. R.J. and myself were as single as single gets, so we had nothing better to do than to try and communicate with and find out what kind of spooks lingered throughout Courtney's house. We did not plan for what we found, and things got very real very quickly.

Throughout the night's investigation, we captured almost a dozen unexplainable audio sounds with our recorders, but did not know about them until we sat down and went through the audio in the days following the investigation. (This is often the case, as voices that are inaudible in real time can be picked up on a recording device.) Nothing happened that was obvious, so we ended up telling stories and having some beers at my brother's house following several hours of investigation.

Beyond the distinct sound of a disembodied motorcycle clearly attempting to start in close proximity to a recorder we had set in the basement and several voices we captured, there was one EVP (electronic voice phenomena) that we caught that chilled us all to the bone.

"Get you dead." [EVP]

I will never forget the first time I heard this eerie voice. The scratchiness of the voice, the matter-of-fact way it came through the recording. Every hair on my body stood on end as this extremely out of place voice came over the recording. The voice did not occur while being questioned, but happened while we were discussing the tragic death of a friend of ours from years earlier. The investigation had ended a while earlier, yet this voice chose that exact time to send the message.

I played this recording for anyone interested in hearing it, and every single person could make out exactly what was said. Everyone who heard it knew this was not one of our voices and was convinced there was a message being sent.

My friend and co-investigator R.J. passed away due to what is called "walking pneumonia" two weeks to the day after we conducted our first and only investigation together.

After we laid R.J. to rest, I knew there was only two ways to take my new passion. Run away as far and fast as I could and chalk this occurrence up as a coincidence and one I never want to talk about or experience again...or dig in and drive forward and no matter what make it my life's goal to help those in need and put everything I have into doing this the way it should be done. I chose the latter and I chose it quickly.

The deciding factor was having a heart-to-heart conversation with the person I knew almost immediately was in many ways a soul mate of mine, Jason.

I knew Jason brought to the table everything necessary: an open and sensitive mind as well as superior technological knowledge. What I didn't know was that he had many years of experience in paranormal research as well as hands-on knowledge and experience with all different types of magick and history of all things paranormal. I knew from the moment he and I spoke about my goals and aspirations, R.J., and everything in between that the two of us could accomplish anything we put our minds to. From that day on, I was determined to make a difference not only in the lives of those we assist, but to make a difference in the field of paranormal research. Jason and I would spend our free time and lives looking for answers and people needing help and doing everything we could to offer our assistance.

Jason and I have a very tight relationship based on our passion for this field of research and trust. There are times I have questioned the things he feels or tells me, but I believe that is healthy. But I have no doubt I can trust his word. If Jason conducts a walk-through of a location, I know it hasn't been contaminated in any way and that I can trust the details he gives me before the investigation begins. He tells me his honest feelings, thoughts, and visions, and I simply make note of them.

The void left in my life and on my new team felt insurmountable, and the thought that this was a horrible idea definitely went through my head. I just could not get that voice out of my head as those words rang through my soul repeatedly.

"Get you dead."

I felt that Jason would be a blessing for all of us, and when he agreed to join us in our quest, I knew we were on the right path. I asked him if he knew anyone who had good camera skills and some interest in joining us in our crazy adventures. Jason did not think for long before he told me he had the perfect person. We set up a meeting at Jason's house for later that evening and my brother and I would go out to discuss our plans and meet Jason's friend Jared.

Snort and I arrive at Jason's house as the sun was going down that evening. Jason welcomed us into his home and we had brought over some new equipment, so we sat down and decided we would just see if everything clicked and go from there. We would start going over some of the big-picture goals and explain what we really wanted to accomplish. Jared arrived shortly after we got there, and Jason introduced my brother and me to him. It felt like the four of us had not even sat down before we had put together an in-depth and incredible plan of action. Jared fit this group like a glove. I explained the big picture ideas that I had and that I would never allow us to waver from that. Unlike the many teams out there that do investigations for the instant payoff, I told them we were going to do this so we could make a difference. I let them all know for sure that they needed to understand that making a difference does not happen overnight. Everyone felt great about our talk and the direction we were heading. I let them know that I would be looking into our options for conducting some investigations together, as I knew we would need some more field experience before we could pursue the type of cases that we really wanted.

Jared brought to the table a great work ethic and attitude. We could all make each other laugh in any situation and we figured that out quickly. He is an incredible photographer and was working on honing his skills with all different types of cameras, so I knew he would be an asset from the very beginning. Jared's sense of humor fit with the rest of us; we knew we could never take ourselves too seriously and had to have fun no matter what. At this point I felt like we were well on our way to moving in the direction I felt we were being called.

Over the next several months we went out as often as we could and had a great time working together. We developed a chemistry that was apparent from our first time in the field.

I knew I would have to make some financial sacrifices in order to work certain types of cases. In most instances, when people invite a team into their home to conduct an investigation, they are looking for some type of validation that the activity they have experienced is real. They are also looking for some type of resolution. I took every last spare dollar I had and invested it in the equipment so we knew we could cover all our bases and give our future clients as much information as possible so they could better understand what may be going on. We had a DVR system that allowed us to set up surveillance cameras throughout a location and we could remotely monitor the area and record video. Our cameras would be set up throughout the location and provided really good night-vision capabilities that we did not otherwise have without using flashlights. We also had a multitude of digital audio recorders that allowed us to document all conversations we had with the clients and the investigations themselves. These pieces of equipment give us the ability to capture EVP throughout the location, which sometimes helps give us a better idea of what we are dealing with, as something could present itself audibly even though we may not be able to hear the message until we review our data following the investigation. We also deploy several different types of EMF (electromagnetic field) detectors. These gauges record spikes in the electromagnetic energy field that shows up naturally all over the place. While sweeping a location with these meters, we can also see where there are man-made magnetic fields that can also contribute to someone having feelings commonly attributed to paranormal activity. Something like a refrigerator, microwave, or old wiring may put out a high level of electromagnetic energy that can sometimes cause a person to feel faint or paranoid—feelings that can be confused with experiencing something paranormal. Measuring these magnetic fields beforehand can help determine the difference between paranormal activity and someone's natural reaction to an EMF. So these meters give us a really good idea what type of a location's baseline energy and allow us to find natural explanations for some seemingly unnatural occurrences.

Another piece of equipment in our arsenal is known as a "Ghost Box." This box sweeps through radio frequencies at a rate of speed that allows for a constant flow of white noise. In theory, this white noise gives any spirits that may be present the ability to communicate with us by speaking through the white noise. This gives us the ability to hear something in real time that may be attempting to talk to us. The speed at which the box sweeps through the frequencies allows words to be formed. The trick is determining what is radio interference and what may be spirit interaction. There are occasions where we receive what sounds like full sentences that come through the box. The fact that the box will have cycled through dozens of channels in that time makes these types of interactions very compelling when pointing toward possible spirit communication.

As we were quickly collecting equipment that would allow us to conduct thorough investigations, I came to a decision to affiliate our team with the Everyday Paranormal organization. They came across to me as very cutting-edge and were in this field for most of the reasons I was. I felt like this would be a good fit for us as we grew and gained experience. They were looking for state affiliates for their organization, so I applied with them and we became the Missouri State affiliate of Everyday Paranormal. I knew this was not a long-term thing, but to this day believe it was a good decision because it helped us begin to really understand where our priorities as a team should lie. In my mind, I knew in what direction I wanted this to ultimately go, however, it would take time. It would take probably years of working together and gaining a true understanding of what we needed to accomplish before really taking the next step. All too often, I see teams pop up out of nowhere and claim to be an experienced and do-gooder type of team, but nine times out of ten they are completely disorganized and have more internal issues than most of the people they claim they are "helping." I knew we needed to avoid this, so we took our growth and public outreach slowly. I wanted to know what we were all made of before we made any claims as to what we were about. I simply asked one thing of my team: trust me. They have trusted me for a long time, and now we are very close to what was the ultimate goal years ago.

Two

THE CASE

The case that changed the lives of many came about just a year and a half or so after we had begun working as a team.

I opened my inbox to see if I had received an email I had anticipated for the last couple days. I was told by a friend in Louisiana that a local Missouri man had inquired about possibly having someone conduct an investigation at his cousin's home. I told her to put the family in touch with me and that I would be happy to evaluate the situation and decide whether or not we needed to proceed with an investigation. There is always a sense of excitement when a new case comes along. This feeling was no different as I opened the email that had shown up as promised.

"My cousin lives in a house that he is afraid to be in anymore. He was recently hospitalized after falling and hitting his head at the top of his basement stairs while doing laundry. He claims to have been attacked by something after the basement door swung open on its own. For a long time now, there have been many people that have had different experiences in the house. Seeing people, hearing footsteps and banging sounds throughout the house are very common. He does not know what is being communicated to him or if something just wants him out of the house. He has lived in the house on his own for about a year. Please understand we do not have much money so we can't pay you for an investigation, but would you be willing to come down and investigate his house to help put his mind at ease? Thank you, Sincerely, Tony"

Never had it crossed my mind to charge anybody money to conduct an investigation. Upon doing a little research, I found that this family had been given an "estimate" by two different "teams" to come in and help them. I couldn't imagine going into someone's home without any guarantees of answers or corrective action and actually forcing them to give me money. There were several more contacts with Tony before we headed down to a small town just outside of Jefferson City, the capital city of Missouri. This area of the state is known for its history and is a very beautiful place with rolling hills and thick woodlands. In this part of Missouri, you really do not have to look very hard to find incredible stories of history and mysterious occurrences.

By the time I took this case, my team and I had worked several private residence cases and felt very confident we would, if nothing else, be able to let this man know if he had anything going on inside his home and whether it was something to be fearful of. I did not realize this case would change my life on many levels.

Tony had explained to me that his cousin, Shane, was deaf. He had been born this way and never had the ability to hear. Something in this house was becoming more and more brazen as the days went by, and because Shane had recently been injured by what Tony told me was some type of spirit, I knew we needed to get down there quickly to see what was really going on.

When we met as a team, I explained that this was a case of a man who was not only afraid for his own safety, but actually felt he had been attacked and subsequently hospitalized as a result of something he claimed to be "evil" viciously coming after him. Everyone seemed calm enough and ready to take on this new challenge. I met with Jason separately.

"All I am going to tell you about this place is it is just outside of Jeff City and involves a man with special circumstances, and we need to get down there to find out what is going on," I said to Jason as he listened intently. I saw a strange look on his face as I spoke to him; it was obvious to me that he was keeping something inside and my guess is he did not want to say out loud what was weighing on his mind.

"She is waiting for you," Jason told me with a very serious face.

"Who?"

"I don't know, but she is eager for you to be there," he continued.

"Are you picking anything else up?" I always get curious when Jason tells me anything about a location we have yet to even step foot into because more often than not, he is spot on.

"Something bad happened there, and there is definitely something else. I can't see it, but something bad is going on," Jason said, reaching into his depths for more information but could only leave my wandering thoughts with this vague and grim nugget of information.

I made note of the idea that this lady was anxiously anticipating our arrival as well as whatever may have been waiting or have happened that was so negative. I have received information from Jason prior to many cases, so I have a good idea how to interpret his communications, but this time felt a little different. He seemed drained from a simple discussion about the vague details of an upcoming case. He almost looked nervous. This was new.

I knew something was waiting for us; I simply did not comprehend the magnitude of what it was and how it would change my overall outlook on not only investigating the paranormal, but on life and death in general. I know now as I tell this story that I will never be the same as I was before I pursued my calling. I struggle from time to time with knowing in my heart whether it is worth giving a piece of my soul to every case I work. I come up with the same exact answer every single time while I weigh the positive and negative that faces me.

Yes, without question. I believe with every fiber of my being that the answer is yes.

Regardless of what may have been waiting for us, we would pack up our gear on the coming weekend and head to the depths of the Show Me State and do whatever we could to help this man and his family find answers. I had developed a much better understanding of the negative effect these things could have on people and their everyday lives. These dark forces can alter someone's ability to function on a daily basis and can ruin lives and relationships. I attempted to prepare myself and my team for whatever may have been waiting, but we all knew in our hearts that there was no way to know exactly what we were getting ourselves into. There was a heavy feeling when it came to discussing the upcoming investigation. It was as though we all knew that in some way there would be some intense times ahead. But this is what we had signed up for. We would set our trepidations aside and pursue answers for this family.

Three

THE HOUSE

It was a warm Saturday in July when we finished packing up our gear and Snort, Jason, Jared, and I headed toward the heart of Missouri. My gut told me that we were in for an interesting evening. All I knew about this case was what I had been told, so I had thought a lot about the special circumstances we would be dealing with.

We opted to tackle this case with our typical approach when we arrived at the house so everybody would know their roles. Jared would accompany me on the initial walkthrough as my brother Snort and Jason got all the gear ready. Keeping Jason away from the initial walk-through was important because once I am familiar with the house and its stories, I conduct another walk with him. For this, we wanted him to have a fresh, unbiased perspective. We were rolling through the hills of Missouri and pulled into a small town just west of Jefferson City and were only a few minutes away. I noticed Jason had quietly become un-comfortable, or had an uncomfortable demeanor. This was not entirely unheard of, as he would sometimes pick up on certain things and usually keep them to himself knowing damn well if he asked me about anything, he would be told basically to wait.

There was a serious look on his face as we approached the house. I turned my attention to the two-story Victorian-style house that looked very similar to most of the sur-rounding homes. It was not small and not a mansion; it was just a house. From the minute I got out of the car, I felt something was out of place. I did not know if it was the jitters of investigating this location for the first time or if it was happening because something out of the ordinary was going on. Jared and I approached the house and were greeted by Tommy, a large and aloof cat that typically hung out on the front porch, but under no circumstances could Tom be coerced into stepping paw inside the house.

The lot the house stood on was larger than those sur-rounding it, probably a double lot, which of course led to there being a large yard. Jason seemed to be immediately drawn to a tree that was standing a little ways from the house, so as Jared and I entered the home to conduct our walk-through, I noted that Jason was working his way toward the tree.

Shane's mother, Debbie, answered the door and greeted Jared and me as we walked through the front door. Debbie was accompanied by Shane, who looked very happy to have us there. He was obviously excited to have someone come into the house that might be able to help him. Debbie explained to me that Shane's cousin Tony and his two friends were around the house as well, so we knew who all was present before we really got started on our walk-through.

"Hello, I am Debbie, Shane's mother. It's nice to meet you," she said in a warm and welcoming Southern accent.

"Hi Debbie. It's nice to finally meet you in person," I returned the salutations and added a handshake.

Shane and I had exchanged a firm handshake and we had decided to communicate with one another through text messages. "Hello, thank you for coming to my house," Shane communicated as he shook my hand and embraced me in a hug.

I knew I would like Shane from the minute I laid eyes on him. He had a very honest look about him and was eager to find help. He was very quick to take Jared and me on the tour. I immediately noticed the home's outrageous décor. It was very apparent that Shane had a lot of cowboy in him and loved the state of Texas. There was something eerie yet endearing about the place. I looked into the living room and coming out of the wall there was woodwork that resembled the outside of a saloon. I knew this would be interesting. Shane explained that he had done all the woodwork himself and was quite proud of it. I could understand why. It wasn't exactly the style I would choose, but the work itself was quite impressive.

Debbie explained to Jared and me that their family had owned this home on two different occasions over the course of about thirty years. She had sold the house about ten years prior to our visit and the family had decided to repurchase the house about three years before they reached out to us. When not under family ownership, the house had been abandoned. She let us know that everyone had been afraid to stay in the house because of the constant activity. They would hear footsteps going up and down the stairs and walking throughout the house. Objects would regularly be moved from one location to another and doors would open and close on their own. She said that the family had had enough, but Shane had decided he was not bothered by the incidents and wanted to make the house his home. She explained that since most of the activity was audible, Shane would likely not be bothered because he could not hear it anyway.

I asked Debbie a series of questions as is typical just so I could get a better idea of what kind of experiences they had had over the years. She provided information that led me to believe they were experiencing a lot of sounds being made throughout the house and occasionally seeing things out of the corner of their eye, things like that. I asked her one question and her answer sank in pretty deeply:

"So have you all ever had anyone come into the house before to attempt to cleanse or investigate further to see what is really going on?" I asked Debbie.

"Yes, actually, about four months ago we convinced our local pastor to come to the house to perform a blessing, and he only made it about halfway through the blessing process before he became violently ill and had to step out of the house. He left after feeling sick and has not come back since, even though we asked him to tell us his thoughts. He just ignores the situation," Debbie told me, with a concerned look on her face.

"Okay, so the pastor will not discuss anything with you or come back to finish the blessing? Has anything changed since that happened here in the house?" I asked.

"Yes, right after the pastor left, things got a lot worse. Almost as though we angered something. The pastor will not talk to me about this anymore and will not come back to the house," Debbie said.

Shane then led us up the stairs, as he wanted to show me a few things on the top floor. As we reached the top of the stairs, he pointed to what was obviously an attic opening and let me know this was a place he would never go. He took us into the room that opened up from the end of the hallway.

"This room is where he sees shadows darting from one end of the hallway into this room," Debbie began to explain.

"There is something about the closet that creeps every-body out," she continued as Shane began to look more and more nervous. He seemed very on edge at this point, so I walked into the room and look into the closet. It seemed like a normal enough closet.

The main thing I had noticed from the minute we stepped inside was the overwhelming pungent odor that filled the house. Obviously there were several cats here and it was even more obvious that they were tended to rarely. There was cat hair and the smell of excrement all over the place. I was told that there hadn't been a lot of cleaning going on lately because of the uptick in activity through-out the home. Nobody felt safe there, so they pretty much kept their distance. The cats had overrun the house and the smell was overpowering.

I made note of the fact that very often in my experi-ence, when we are called into homes to investigate para-normal activity, most of the homes tend to be in a state of either disrepair or neglect. It is theorized that dark or op-pressive energy can be very attracted to, or even strength-ened in, an environment where the living people have lost control of the surroundings. I have seen instances in which people that would be considered hoarders have claimed to be surrounded by loads of paranormal activity in their home. There is the well-known saying "Cleanliness is next to Godliness." I actually believe there is something to that. Thinking about having to live in filth all the time is something I could not handle. I was told that nobody consistently lived in this house, which was the main reason why it had not been cleaned very well. The few parts of the house where people spent most of their time were definitely much cleaner than the rest of the place.

We continued our tour of the upstairs as we walked into the adjoining room that we referred to as the "nursery." Debbie had mentioned that she was told a story about a small child who had gotten very sick and eventually died as she inhabited the room. The next room was an office space where Shane had set up his computer. He immediately walked over to the computer and started shaking the monitor violently. Debbie interrupted, "Things in this room move quite often. The monitor was shaken violently as he was sitting at the desk working on the computer."

As the demonstration went on with the monitor being shaken violently, Jared and I shared a quick glance and began to wonder what we would be told next. As we went into the final room, aside from the bathroom, Shane began to spin a chair and we were informed the chair had a tendency to spin on its own. It was a normal chair with wheels; Jared and I could see how someone might think the chair could spin by itself if one of the cats happened to be lying on it and jumped off quickly. We knew there was a possible reason for the report, but decided to mark a spot in this room to set up a still camera to see if we could capture the chair in action.

I followed Shane into the bathroom and before I really knew what was going on, Shane looked back at me and screamed, "Beeeeeeeeeehhhhhhhhhhhh!!!!" at the top of his lungs. I was pretty sure I needed a change of pants as he scared the shit out of me when he yelled for no reason at all. At this point, he was shaking and becoming extremely agitated. Debbie began to explain to me this was the room where Shane had heard the only thing he had ever heard in his life.

"He was taking a shower one morning and while he was in there, there was a long and blood-curdling scream in his ear." Debbie began to tear up slightly as she explained that the only noise Shane had ever heard in his entire life was something so frightening.

"Is that even possible?" I asked Debbie.

"Not to my knowledge, but he has always seemed traumatized since that happened," Debbie told me as she got a little choked up. Knowing the one thing her son had heard was so frightening was obviously too much for her to bear.

"If he were to be able to hear something, would it be more likely that he would hear something on a very low frequency or a very high frequency?" I asked Debbie to try to understand any potential of something like this really happening.

"If anything, I would guess it would be a much lower frequency," Debbie said.

"Understood. I'm sorry that happened. I can only imagine," I told Debbie as I noted the fact that EVPs are typically captured on a frequency lower than what is audible for people with normal hearing. I wondered if there could be some type of connection between Shane hearing something so clearly and what we might capture with our recorders, so I knew we would have to focus on the information our recorders provided.

Shane led us out of the bathroom, and, as the family went downstairs, Jared and I stayed behind under the guise of scouting equipment setup to assess the situation. They had explained that they also constantly saw and heard things on the stairs. So far, a lot of activity had been reported, and we had not even made it halfway through the house. We could not figure out if this might be due to overactive imaginations or the fact that things had gotten blown out of proportion because they were so freaked out. We vowed to keep an open mind.

Regardless of the reason, it had become clear very quickly why this family refused to stay in this house on a nightly basis—they were afraid. Debbie had lived there for years and could no longer tolerate the strange happenings, and they were under the impression that Shane would not be as bothered because he could not hear anything. As Jared and I met back up with them in the kitchen, it became clear this was not accurate.

As we entered the kitchen, we met a few more people who had been walking around the basement area and the lower level as we were being shown the upstairs. A girl, probably in her early twenties, walked right by Jared and me and left through the front door. I quickly acquainted myself with her friend, a girl named Audrey, and Shane's cousin Tony, who had initially contacted us for help. I shook hands with Tony and we exchanged pleasantries. He said he needed to go outside and check on his friend, as she was feeling sick to her stomach.

As Jared, Debbie, Shane, and I stood in the kitchen, the environment made me a little uneasy, as the decorations of small trinkets and cowboy decorations were a little much. There was an old-fashioned feel to it, but as we were being told story after story about the strange things going on in the house, the fact that it was decorated in such a loud manner was a little odd. Debbie then told me the main reason they as a family had decided to contact us and ask for help. Shane grabbed a drill and began to remove two wooden planks that had been nailed to the basement door since the attack.

"Shane was in here (pointing to the laundry room next to the basement door) doing laundry one morning and suddenly he noticed the basement door latch had come undone," Debbie said. There was a traditional latch that allowed you to lock the basement door and would have been very difficult to move by itself. You had to lift up and slide the lock in order for it to come undone.

"As he came over to see what had happened, the door slowly creaked open and when he stood in front of the door, it flew open with force and startled him so much he stepped back and tripped. He fell down and hit his head and blacked out for a spell," Debbie continued.

As Debbie was explaining the story, Shane stood in the doorway and acted out what had happened. He was very animated because he wanted to make his point clear. And to show that he was not crazy, he needed to show us exactly what had happened.

"As he came to, he was lying right here (Debbie pointed to the kitchen floor) and Toby (the cat…more on Toby later) was lying on his chest looking up and his hair was standing on end. As he came back into focus with his eyes, he noticed above him were four shadows floating around him in circles. Toby was hissing loudly and swiping in an upward direction as though he were trying to protect Shane," Debbie explained nervously.

"Toby screamed one last time and swiped into the air and all four shadows flew back down the basement stairs faster than he could blink. That is when he got to his feet and locked the door," Debbie told me as Shane got very animated about slamming the door shut and locking the latch. He also showed me this was exactly why he'd had to nail the two boards across the basement door. They let us know the boards had been put up the day this happened and had not been removed since.

"He spent three days in the hospital with a concussion and didn't want to come back here again, so we decided it was time to get in touch with someone to see if we can find some kind of answers. I don't want anyone to be in danger, and Shane doesn't feel comfortable staying here alone anymore," Debbie said in a sweet, soft tone.

"I understand. If something like that happened to me, I doubt I would want to stay in the house anymore either," I said to Debbie while looking Shane in the eye and nodding in understanding. He and I had decided it would be easier to communicate by text messages, so if he had to make a point, he would message me.

Shane took Jared and me into his room on the main level. Again, we saw more of his incredibly artistic woodwork on his bed frame and on the accompanying wall. It again looked like the outside of a saloon.

"Someone walks back and forth along the wall next to my bed all the time," Shane explained to me as he pointed to the wall that had not always stood where it was presently located.

He had told me about waking up from a deep sleep and feeling like something was pressing down on top of him. Some people theorize that is a form of sleep paralysis, which I believe to be one possibility. The way he described it to me was like very strong hands pressing on his chest and he was unable to move any of his limbs. What was odd was the fact that he specifically pointed out while that several times it was happening he would feel a subtle breeze in his face as, as though someone was breathing into his face.

It was time for the last portion of the walk-through and Debbie had told me she refused to go downstairs. She had apparently abandoned the idea of going down there for any reason several years prior to the latest incident involving Shane. Shane led the way, slowly, followed by me and Jared.

We made our way down each steep, creaky step toward the basement. I slowly made my way down, trying to avoid hitting my head on the overhanging wall positioned immediately below the stairs that lead to the upstairs level. With each passing CREAK I can see more and more of this dilapidated and ignored section of the home. The concrete floor was covered with all kinds of debris. There were chairs, pieces of wood, and an immeasurable number of other random things cluttering up what would be the large open area of this basement. As I made my way to the bottom of the stairs, I look back and look right through the back of the staircase, expecting some creature to pop up out of nowhere and reach through the openings as if it had been under these stairs for countless days just rotting away.

I noticed the room located in front of me as I stand at the base of the stairs. Just to my left was a door that opens, as if this small, dark enclosure is inviting me in. My eyes went past all the debris in the main area as I look at the very large and very old-looking furnace. My first thought was "I could put something very large in there, for sure." Just beyond my immediate view of the furnace was a concrete wall that protruded from the opposite wall of the basement. It stood about four feet high and jutted out from the foundation wall about six feet. Very random. My gaze continued toward the back of the basement behind the random wall and the furnace and as I looked through all the cobwebs that have collected over years of neglect. I saw another foundation wall that had large cracks all throughout. I noted that this wall stood about five feet high and behind it was dirt. I worked my way back to this wall to investigate further, wondering if I might find is anything of note. I removed the webs with my hands as I slowly made my way to the back of the basement, noting a crunch beneath my feet with every ginger step I took. I approached the wall and peered behind, only to see nothing but dirt in every direction as the floor to the main level stood just another foot and a half or so above the layer of dirt. I couldn't help but wonder what I might find if I were to climb back there and do some digging. The only question was whether or not I had the balls to do it.

As I got back to area by the basement stairs, I stood soaking in my surroundings and noticed a small dirty window on the wall to my left. Jared and I worked our way over the soggy floor and loose boards that were spread all over the basement. Shane pointed toward the tiny room, and Jared and I worked our way toward it. I felt like we were making our way toward a jail cell. We slowly made our way over to some fallen pieces of plywood and placed a couple of them over some small puddles of muddy water that had likely accumulated from a recent rainstorm. This basement did not come across as one impervious to leaks. After covering up the puddles, we slowly made our way into the room.

Upon entering the tiny room, we noticed several things immediately. There was odd artwork all over the walls that the family had claimed to have had nothing to do with. I also noticed some odd scratches in the walls. The ceiling stood about six and a half feet, so we were very cramped and the room felt a bit like a tomb. I noticed a small drain near one corner, but the artwork and scratches were my biggest concern. Shane pointed to six candles that sat on the floor because they spooked him—he believed they had belonged to whoever was responsible for the artwork.

I asked Shane if he or anyone else who had lived there had ever kept any kind of animal in the room, but Shane responded that no one had animals. These scratches were fairly consistent, always in sets of three and ranging from two to four inches in length. I ran my fingers over several sets of them and noticed they were fairly deep in the concrete wall. I was trying to come up with an explanation for how so many of these scratches would be embedded into the wall. What did they mean? What caused them? They seemed to look like the work of a raccoon, but there was no way a raccoon could have reached the height of some of the scratch marks, so I was left to wonder.

The artwork was strange, and there were a few things on the walls that really stood out. First, just below the window previously mentioned, there were vertical lines that seemed to be stained into the wall. They covered only the area just below the window but ran all the way to the floor. Toward the top of these lines were horizontal lines that created almost a checkerboard look, but it seemed odd that the only place the lines were present in the entire room was just below this seemingly useless window. In fact, the entire room seemed useless to me. As I looked to the connecting wall, there was a very obvious symbol. It looked like two lightning bolts intertwined making the shape of an S, this was a symbol used in Nazi Germany that stands for *Schuttzstaffel*, or "Protective Echelon," in English. It was originally used by Adolf Hitler for his small bodyguard unit, which eventually grew into the force that served as his army.

I recognized this symbol and wondered why on earth it was embedded into this wall. There was nothing else on the walls that would indicate some kind of supremacist had lived here. Shane did love the South, but I never came across anything indicating he was an extremist.

One of the other things that stood out was the fact that there were about a half-dozen handprints imprinted into the wall. They were not in the mold as though you see initials sometimes marked in concrete as it dries, and they were not painted on the wall. It was just very strange. They were there and there were no fingerprints or anything, simply the shape of hands.

The last thing I noticed quickly was on the low ceiling was a clear marking of what is known as the "Eye of Ra." Again, it was a very recognizable symbol throughout the world that seems to have different meanings in different societies. Many cultures throughout the world have the symbol of an eye overlooking people. I did not know whether this was a symbol placed on the ceiling of this room to represent a form of protection or if it had more sinister meaning. Symbolic intent aside, this was quite clearly an eye looking down upon anyone standing in this room. This, of course, created a rather uncomfortable feeling. I knew I would be curious to get Jason's take on this room was when he did his walk-through. This is the type of symbol he is very familiar with on many levels, so I waited to hear his take on why it was there and how it got there.

I began to ask Shane a series of questions about all the markings on the walls and whether or not he or his family may have had anything to do with them. He vehemently denied any involvement and was very strong on his stance that nobody had been down in this basement for a very long time. Since they re-purchased the house three years ago, he said nobody had used the basement. He was unsure how all these markings had come to be, so for all we knew, the markings could have been there for a very long time. It would be next to impossible to know for sure.

At this point, Jared and I concluded the walk-through and thanked everyone for their help and their taking the time to tell the stories that could be relevant in our investigation. I explained to Shane and Debbie that I would do everything possible to help them find answers and, hopefully, a solution. I told Shane he was welcome to come back by after a few hours to join in with us so we could see if there was any difference when he was there and when he was not.

I spoke to Tony and asked him if his friend was feeling better. He said she felt fine as soon as she left the house. He had been curious of my opinion of the room, so I told him there is definitely a creepy vibe. When I mentioned the scratches on the wall in the basement room as something that really stood out, he gave me a blank look and asked what I was talking about. I told him they were very obvious, and he asked me to accompany him downstairs to take a look. He was followed by Audrey and as we walked into the basement room, Audrey let out a quick half-scream and stopped herself from losing her composure.

"What's the matter?" I asked curiously.

"Dude, I swear to God, those were not there when we were in here just a little bit ago before you guys came downstairs," Tony said, as all the color quickly drained from his face and Audrey quickly left the basement.

"No shit," I said matter-of-factly, feeling quite skeptical, but keeping in mind that I really did not know these people.

Tony, Debbie, and I did have a quick talk about the house and its history. They made it clear that they were attempting to distance themselves from the house because there seemed to be a stigma attached to it throughout their small community. They felt they were the subject of widespread gossip and judgment, and they believed wholeheartedly that it had a lot to do with the house.

But they were all very fond of the house and were having a difficult time completely letting it go, as though it would just draw them back in. At this point, they were all afraid of the house, and they let me know they simply hoped to find out if whatever was there could be removed and whether or not people were safe inside the home.

Our initial walk-through had ended and there was something very different about this house that I could not put my finger on. I could not wait for our scheduled walk-through to see what Jason felt. Something in the pit of my stomach told me we were in for something, though I had no idea what. Regardless of whether some of the stories we had been told were fabricated, something was going on in that house.

I asked Debbie and Shane about Tommy and Toby, as both cats definitely had a personality about them. I thought it was very interesting that both cats were quickly pointed out before and during the walk-through. The house was not maintained well, so I wanted to get more information on both cats.

It is widely believed that animals have heightened senses that can allow them to see, feel, and hear things that humans typically cannot. I have seen many things that lend credibility to the idea that animals, for example, will act differently in the time leading up to a large natural disaster, many animals will act differently. They know and can feel something different, sometimes noting that something is not right or is out of place, so they react accordingly.

Shane moved into the house that his mother had recently moved out of knowing about all the stories and history. Shane, being a pretty tough-minded individual felt he
would be fine because he was a total skeptic when it came
to ghosts or anything out of the ordinary. After all, Shane
had lived a very different life than most people and dealt
with many hardships because of his handicap. Only the
hearing-impaired can imagine what it is like growing up in
a small town where most people seem to know one another.
Shane had been through a lot in his life and was ready to
take on more responsibility and own his own house, so he
didn't hesitate when the opportunity presented itself.

On the day Shane brought Toby and Tommy to the
house, he noticed something different about them. Their
demeanor immediately changed. He had mostly finished
unpacking and wanted to set up the house so they would
feel at home. Toby became very edgy when he was brought
into the house, and Tommy acted strangely too. Rather
than coming along peacefully to see the wonders of his
new abode, he instead gashed Shane's arm near where he
held him in such a panic that he flipped him away from his
chest to tend to his now bleeding wound. Tommy bolted
faster than lightning toward the front door and never set
one paw inside the house again. Tommy did not leave
(he was very loyal), but he found his home on the front
porch and refused to so much as entertain the idea of ever
being taken into that house again. Even through the win-
ter months and harsh summers, there Tommy remained,

steady. Tommy had never been what most would consider an "outdoor" cat prior to Shane's move into the family house. Now, he simply made his home as the protector of his master on the porch. He would venture out into the yard on occasion, but spent the vast majority of his days and nights perched on the stone wall standing in front of the house, as though he was warning anyone and everyone that would listen to stay out of the house.

Toby was a little more adventurous than Tommy, and he accompanied his friend and owner into the belly of the beast, so to speak. Toby was smaller than Tommy, but had a personality that was very apparent and brazen. He was as sweet as can be and sociable when it came to interacting with people. He let his opinion be known whenever the situation called for it though. When Shane was home, Toby spent the majority of his time keeping an eye on him and staying in close proximity to him. He did this as though he were a well-trained guard dog, protecting his master.

When Shane would leave, Toby would typically disappear into Shane's room and be seen much less often. Toby would interact with other people as long as there was someone in the house, and he seemed as normal as any cat can. He was very friendly and cordial to all of us as we inhabited the house, even when Shane was gone. Toby did not mind us wandering around the house, upstairs or throughout the main level of the home, but when we ventured to the basement, his tone and overall demeanor changed drastically.

No matter who it was, if anyone opened the basement door, Toby would appear seemingly out of nowhere and begin voicing his displeasure with that person in every way he knew how. He would stand at your feet and let out meows that sounded more like screaming or crying. He would circle you in an attempt to persuade you to close the door and walk in the opposite direction. He would habitually jump a step or two down the stairs toward the basement as any person made their way toward the bottom of the stairs in an effort to turn them around. He absolutely refused to leave any person down in the basement by themselves. He would stand strong by the person and spend the entire time trying to convince anyone down there to turn back.

Four

Jason's Walk

As usual, I cleared everyone else from the house and asked Jason to walk through the house with me and tell me what he felt. This helps on a number of levels, but mostly it lets me see if what he feels correlates with any of the claims made by the people who live there on a daily basis. Sometimes the results can be unnerving. I try to keep any reaction to myself as Jason does his walk so as to not push him in any particular direction.

"You ready, buddy?" I asked as Jason began walking toward the house with me.

As he breathed heavily, Jason said, "Something really heavy here. Bad things have happened. I feel like this is a mortuary of sorts ... or has been in the past."

We walked into the house and almost immediately Jason felt the same heaviness that everybody else did. The way the house was set up and decorated could very easily have led someone to conclude that all sorts of odd things were going on. He took deep breath after deep breath as we made our way upstairs. He walked toward the corner room by the scratching post and the stench of cat excrement was powerful. He walked in and said that a child had passed there. This was the main thing he felt while going through the three rooms upstairs. He did point out that the attic space had a distinct feel coming from it, and that it was not positive. As he walked into the bathroom upstairs, he said, "Something enjoys tormenting people in this house, especially in here."

"Powerful and mischievous are two words that come to mind. This thing has potential to hurt someone badly and it feeds off someone's disability. It likes to be vocal and physical because it affects someone closely," he continued, as we head back down the stairs. While on the stairs, Jason paused and claimed, "Heavy traffic area. Up and down the stairs all the time; it isn't just one thing. There is a man and woman that go up and down the stairs often, as well as a child. And the other thing: It feels like this house is one big portal, almost like things come and go as they please, although some of them cannot leave."

I paused because this was an exact match of what we had been told about the stairs—the many claims of almost constant sounds of people walking or running up and down the stairs. Jason had also pointed out in the bathroom the fact that whatever was lingering in the house made a point to make itself clearly known while Shane was in the shower. The information about the child passing was something I was unsure of. We would have to do some research to see if this was fact or fiction.

We made our way back down to the main level and Jason paused in the main hallway to point out this whole area was somewhat of a "passage" for many entities. We walked down the hallway to the dining room area just before the kitchen when Jason paused and peeked over his shoulder at the basement door. I could see the color drain from his face. I asked him to keep coming through toward the main bedroom, but he shook it off and came with me after taking one last quick peek at the door. We make our way to the bedroom, and he immediately pointed out someone pacing along the foot of the bed.

"Not to scare someone; this feels more residual. There used to be a door here (pointing at the wall that was previously discussed with Shane) and this man walks back and forth nonstop. He doesn't even know we are here." Then he finished his thought.

"Something else comes in here on occasion though, something comes in to see if it can scare someone and it does. Physical contact is common because it feels that is the easiest way to make an impression," Jason said with no emotion in his tone.

Shane had explained waking up short of breath and feeling as though something was lying on top of him and holding him down. What Jason was saying to me made perfect sense.

After we finished up in the master bedroom, we made our way toward the basement. As I opened the basement door, Jason paused and began to develop issues with his breathing. He had to take long and slow breaths. I have seen this happen during other investigations. He has explained it as a way to keep some distance between himself and something that could potentially attempt to enter him. Under normal circumstances, Jason does not have these issues, but having worked together for a while now, I knew that when he would go into these breathing "trances" he was about to tell me he is feeling something strong. He seemed very uncomfortable, but said we should proceed to the basement.

Jason followed me into the odd, dungeonlike basement room that was said to have been used for séances, which has likely allowed something to gain strength, although that entity had been here long before the séances took place. He said whatever it is typically stays in the basement, but can and does come upstairs on occasion. This is the dark force he had felt on our way here and, and though he was not entirely sure what it is capable of, it did not come across as anything that had ever been human. I took these observations with a grain of salt, but I would be an idiot to dismiss them entirely, as I could feel a distinct difference between the air downstairs and anywhere else in the house. I never assumed any type of activity, specifically "demonic" activity, so I took my notes and realized that this case could be a handful.

"Something has happened down here in the past," Jason said. "I feel like there are many spirits that come through here, some are stuck here and others just pass through. This basement is a highway of activity. I feel like someone was buried down here. Someone that lived here in the past used this basement for shady practices, I just don't know exactly what it is. That is the main reason this dark energy has found a home here."

I just listened as we continued to allow him to pick up on anything that stood out. He made his way to the wall standing toward the back of the basement and then turned his attention to the crawlspace between the foundation of the house and the floor.

"I don't get a good feeling back here at all. I can't put my finger on it, but it feels like someone is trapped here, or an overwhelming feeling of claustrophobia right in this area," Jason said, as his breathing became more labored. The longer we stayed in the basement, the amount of effort to have regular breathing increased.

As we finished up our walk in the basement, we were about to head upstairs to meet with the team so I could take the rest of them through the house and we could begin prepping the investigation. As we approach the stairs there was a sudden CRASH in the room.

We immediately stopped and hustled into the room to see what had happened—there really wasn't anything in there that could have made this sound. As I entered the room, I saw a candle inside a glass casing rolling across the floor. It was one of several candles that had been in the room; there was nothing else in the room at all. I could not think of any reason this candle would have moved, let alone found a way to make such a loud crashing sound. Jason and I look at each other and at this point, we knew this might be a very eventful evening. We would not be disappointed.

Five

SETUP AND INVESTIGATION #1

We rolled out the equipment and started running cables all over the house. I wanted to make sure we had eyes in as many places as possible as well as quality audio. We end up running six infrared cameras throughout the house, which would give us the ability to monitor any movement in the house. We were able to cover the reported hot spots from upstairs (where there seems to be constant movement) to the main floor in the kitchen, master bedroom, and living room areas. Of course, we also placed a couple cameras in the basement, since we already had an instance of an object moving for no apparent reason.

As Jared was setting up the cameras in the basement, Toby, Shane's very protective and obnoxious cat, followed him down. I heard a yell coming from the basement and ran down to check on Jared, who told me that Toby had scared the shit out of him and would not get out from under his feet as he was trying to set up the camera. I of course, got a good chuckle out of this. Jared was still very new to the investigation process, but was very talented when it came to setting up the equipment and using a camera. He had immediately proven himself a valuable member of the team...and of course was always good for a laugh or two during an investigation.

After we got all the cameras and audio set up on this hot evening in central Missouri, we prepared ourselves to expect the unexpected. I had decided to place everyone strategically throughout the house to begin our first attempt at communication, and we geared up and made sure there was plenty of caffeine to go around. We were ready, and we had high hopes we could help Shane figure out what the hell is going on in his house.

Jared started upstairs with Jason, and my brother Snort was manning the main level as I headed downstairs by myself. Well, mostly by myself; Toby decided he needed to join me downstairs as well. He got more and more vocal with each step I took down the creaky staircase that led to the abyss of the basement. I noted that Toby seemed to be very irritable with anyone who wanted to head to the basement. This was the third time he had let his opinion be heard when someone tried to go downstairs, so this struck me as very odd. He acted completely normal when interacting with all of us anywhere else in the house, but when it came to the basement, he was extremely edgy. I made the decision to allow Toby to wander through the house as he saw fit unless it became unbearable. For the most part, he would stay out of our way, but I wanted to give him the chance to show me what he may know about what is going on in the house, as he kept the "suck factor" to a minimum.

The sun had set, and I sat quietly in the basement's dungeon room simply trying to take in my surroundings and began asking the usual simple questions we used to start most investigations. The EVP activity began almost immediately, as I would learn shortly thereafter upon playing back and reviewing my recorders.

"We have been asked to come here to find answers for Shane, do you know Shane?" I asked as I began to feel more and more uncomfortable in the room. I have felt this way before, but almost never just after the investigation begins.

"Is there a message you would like to send to Shane? I can hear you, he cannot; you know this, tell me what your message is," I continued.

"Fuck Shane … leave!" [EVP]

I noted the temperature on my gauge dropped slightly from 83 to 81, and a few seconds later I noted the temperature gauge showed 78 and I could physically feel the coolness of the air. There were no windows and absolutely no air movement in this basement room, I noted this on my recorder. It was a very warm evening and we had turned off all A/C units in the house almost two hours ago. Again, there was no logical reason for the temperature to suddenly change. I received radio contact from Jason and Jared upstairs:

"It feels like it is getting cool up here. I was hot and now it feels like the air conditioning is on. You turned it off, right?"

"Yeah, we turned off all A/C units almost two hours ago. I just registered a drop from 83 to 78 and it is sitting at 76 and dropping steadily, give me a minute." I let them know I needed a few minutes of radio silence.

First 74, then 72, then 69.5. The temperature kept steadily dropping.

"Are you making the temperature drop? Is this your way of telling me something?" I asked quietly.

66.6 steady.

"My house." [EVP]

"Can you keep the temperature where it is now? Do you feel like these numbers have significance?" I asked.

As the temperature in the basement room remained steady on the Mel-Meter at 66.6, there was a spike in EMF reading that went from 0.1 mG to 6.6 and then held steady. I was astonished to see for a period of about 30 seconds an EMF level of 6.6 and a temperature reading of 66.6 degrees and I knew something out of the ordinary was going on. All this happening within 20 minutes of beginning our first investigation. It was obvious that something needed our attention and had a message to get across to all of us, as my recorder picked up a very clear EVP.

(*Woman's voice*) *"Danger... please go."* [EVP]

This EVP was almost overpowered by another voice that simultaneously said:

"Mine... go... now." [EVP]

Radio contact from Jason and Jared again:

"This place is freaking creepy... now it feels warm again up here," Jason said.

"Totally quiet here fellas," Snort chimed in.

"I can't even explain what was just going on, you'll have to see it for yourself, I need to check the audio," I told everyone.

I began to review on recorder that was present during the first Q&A session and find several EVPs, including those described herein. I was floored and excited at the same time. I made a point to gather with the guys to let them know what I had discovered. I knew this would allow us to push forward with the investigation and make sure we kept our line of questioning consistent because it seemed like several entities were attempting to contact us. Everybody was at a loss for words when we discussed what we had already caught and having just begun.

We decided to continue changing positions around the house so everyone could get a taste of all the main areas that were reported hotspots. The basement continued to be the main area of an overwhelming feeling of despair and agitation. When Snort was down there, he had an experience with Jason.

"So you can change the temperature in the room? It's kind of hot right now, can you cool us off a little?" Snort asked.

At this moment, his flashlight turned on from the holster on his belt loop. It is a twist-top mini-Maglite and should certainly not come on by itself, specifically while in the off position. At this time, he also felt a brush against his back.

"What the hell?! Something just ran its fingers down my back!" Snort said.

"Dude, your flashlight is on! Haha!" As only Jason can do, in his excitement he finds this endlessly entertaining.

As this is going on downstairs, Jared and I heard a thump coming from the top of the stairs as we were in the master bedroom, and we moved in to investigate.

"Wait! Do you feel that??" I asked Jared, stopping dead in my tracks in the main hallway just next to the staircase.

"Whoa! You haven't turned the A/C on at all, right?" Jared asked me.

"No dude, it is absolutely freezing right here! Hold on," I said, as I had Jared stand in a place where the temperature gauge registered 68 degrees in what had been one of the warmest parts of the house all evening. Then I moved about four feet toward the front door and the temperature gauge registered what had been a normal 81 degrees—a 13-degree difference within five feet with no moving air source whatsoever. This was not a breeze; it was stagnant, cold air that simply floated in one location in the hallway as we had been heading toward the staircase to investigate some sounds.

"I'm going upstairs for a second, hold the Mel-Meter while I go check out that noise," I told Jared as he stood in the midst of this chilly spot.

I headed upstairs and found nothing out of place. My handheld equipment registered nothing. The house had been flat when it came to EMF readings all evening, except near the appliances of course. Upstairs everything seemed to be as it was when we left it, so I headed back downstairs. As I neared the bottom of the staircase, Jared was still standing where I had left him and said, "Dude, now it's gone. It just suddenly went back to normal! What the hell?"

"I'm not sure bro. We have recorders running and cameras everywhere though, so hopefully we picked something up," I told him, still unsure of what was going on. At this point, I was feeling like we were receiving signals of sorts, but from whom? From what? I was not even close to understanding what was happening, but there had been many doubts put to rest as to whether Shane and his family were telling the truth about having experiences in this house. There was undoubtedly something out of the ordinary going on.

"Did you brush against anything? Right when you said you got touched, your light turned on! That was flippin' sweet!" a still-excited Jason said to Snort.

"Courtney," a low voice whispers. [DV—Disembodied Voice]

"That is freaking crazy!" Snort responded as he turned his flashlight back to the off position.

We met up in the main level's living room just across the hallway from where we had waded in the cold spot for almost three minutes. We exchanged pleasantries and tales of the insane moments we had experienced in separate rooms and almost exactly at the same time. At this point, we knew something was going on, so we stepped outside to decide how to continue.

"I feel like there is a woman that goes up and down. She feels like an almost protective presence that is interested in what we are doing, as well as concerned," Jason said.

"That isn't it though. I felt creeped out downstairs," I said. "I don't know how else to say it, and that ridiculous cold spot; that was just ridiculous; never seen or heard of anything like that. It was thick and just stayed right where we were, and then was just gone!" I extinguished my cigarette and prepared to head back in.

"We need to get the Ghost Box out and see what happens downstairs. I need to know what the hell is going on down there, so let's see if this bastard can talk through the Box," I said to the crew, and everyone nodded in agreement.

Ghost Box Session in the Basement Room

When this case occurred, the Ghost Box was a fairly new device, at least the device itself, certainly not its function. The concept of spirits having the ability to easily speak through the constant static of radio frequencies flying by at a high rate of speed had been around for quite some time. Because the frequencies changed so often, it was easy to distinguish the difference between radio channels being picked up with partial words and thoughts and what often sounded like full sentences and distinct voices. This invaluable tool could help us determine if there were spirits in the basement room as well as who and what they were doing—in real time. This allowed us to quickly establish a possible motive for the activity going on throughout the house.

"I don't care who or what you are, I don't even care how many of you there are, step forward and speak to us," I began the questioning process. Immediately there were multiple responses.

"Hello?" a female voice inquires. [GB]

"Shhhhh" follows the female voice almost instantaneously. [GB]

"Was that you? Are you a woman? If so, make the lights on the device I am holding blink. I would like to establish communication with you," I said as the lights on my K-II meter immediately illuminate.

"Alright, please step back and make the lights stop blinking. Can you do that?"

"Fuckers!" very clearly sounds from the Ghost Box . . . as the lights on the K-II stop blinking

"Thank you," I said. "Now, can you make three lights go on signifying 'Yes' and two lights go on for signifying 'No?' I asked as three lights went on.

"Sweet!" Jared said as I shushed him. The tension seemed to be building as we had not come across such a willing participant with the ability to so easily manipulate our equipment in quite some time.

"What time, assholes?" came clearly from the Ghost Box. The woman's voice we had heard before seems to have faded, as there was now a more forceful voice that kept coming through.

"Miss, do you know who we are and why we are here?" I asked as the K-II moves to the second light, signaling "No" to that particular question.

"Do you know our names?" I continued, and almost immediately three lights are on as *"Brandon"* clearly came out of the Ghost Box in the same female voice we had heard moments before.

Courtney joined in the conversation, "Do you know anyone else's name?" he asked as three lights came on the K-II meter I was holding and almost immediately from the Ghost Box: *"Snort"* [GB]

"Whoa!!!" We collectively were impressed and a little stunned.

"Are we in trouble?" Snort continued as all the lights on the K-II go crazy and the Ghost Box continues on cue:

"Go now; please" again, the same female voice we had now heard several times. She was asking us to leave and seemed to be pleading her case.

"Do you like it down here in the basement?" I asked as two lights went on, indicating she does not like the basement. I continued, "Is that because something else is down here?" as three lights quickly come on.

"Dude, I feel like she needs us to leave this room; something in here doesn't like her talking with us," Jason said.

At this point, Jared is all but frozen in awe. He was still fairly new to investigating the paranormal and he had never experienced anything like this. To be honest, neither had any of us. It was absolutely remarkable to get responses so quickly not from one, but two pieces of equipment.

Snort had set his flashlight up on the sill of the random and seemingly useless window in this room before we had begun our communication efforts with the Ghost Box, and it suddenly lit up as *"Get out!"* came clearly through the Ghost Box in that familiar and very forceful voice. Again, we were all very excited at this point but a little nervous because we had no idea what we were dealing with, and it did not sound accommodating.

"Miss, can you tell me your name?" I asked, which commanded an immediate response *"Emily"* from the Ghost Box.

"No way!" Jared jumped in as we all looked at each other and confirmed the name we had all just heard. We were still in some disbelief but took it in stride. I asked Emily, "Would you feel more comfortable if we talk to you in another room?" I didn't even get the question entirely out of my mouth before the three lights on the K-II shined brightly. They almost seemed to shine even more brightly than they had before. We turned off the Ghost Box and slowly moved out of the basement room and headed up the stairs. What I didn't realize at the time was that as we were heading up the stairs, one of our static voice recorders picked up an awful growling sound from the room we had just exited. This would damn near give me a heart attack when I reviewed the audio file after this night's investigation. Something very simply did not want us in this house. It didn't want anybody in this house, and we would eventually find this out ourselves.

We reached the top of the stairs and as we opened the door, there was Toby, and he was making it quite clear he was not impressed with our decision to spend time in the basement without him there to supervise, as evidenced by his constant and forceful meowing. There was nothing threatening about his communication; it was just quite obvious that Toby wanted our attention and would not shut up until we gave it to him, so we let Jared pet him while sitting on the couch for a few minutes. We had all gone into the living room to monitor the DVR system we had set up so we could check out all the cameras we had run. We had kept hearing different thumping-type sounds and the occasional scratch throughout the night. It was happening all over the house, so we decided to relax for a few minutes and see if anything happened in the living room area.

I don't know what it was, but something turned my attention near the foot of the staircase where we had heard thumping coming from earlier in the evening. This was just a few feet from where Jared and I experienced the prolonged cold spot that we could not explain. So I slowly and quietly walked over to the foot of the stairs with the intention of taking a picture into the closet to my right, and in my mind's eye I would immediately turn and take a picture to my left that would have led up the staircase. I approached the closet and took the picture, and then as I turned to take the picture up the staircase, there was what appeared to be the chest of a woman right in front of my face. I saw this bosom as clearly as my hand would appear right in front of me. I could make out the ruffles down the center of the blouse and it stunned me so badly I just about killed myself as I nearly jumped back into the closet.

"Oh shit! What the fuck??!!" I was completely out of breath and felt like I just got the shit scared out of me at a haunted house or something. What I had seen was so close to my face and so real, I did not expect it and could not wrap my brain around it.

"What?!" the fellas asked.

"Dude, there was just tits in my face…I shit you not!" My exclamation receives an immediate round of hysterical laughter, but they can all see the terror on my face as I explain further: "Seriously, I turned to take the picture up the stairs and right in my face was a woman's torso wearing what looked like an old blouse. It had ruffles and shit down the middle, but she was right in my face and then as I jumped, she was immediately gone!"

Nobody had ever seen me react like this on any investigation, so they were all highly entertained and interested to know what really just happened. I stood there catching my breath and had Jared toss me the K-II meter. "Was that you Emily?" I asked. I got no response on the K-II, however, on the recorder I had been holding, a very distinct and feminine voice shortly after: *"Hmmm; hi,"* [EVP] she said.

"Alright, if that was you Emily, I am going to come over here and sit down; please come with me. I would like to get to know you," I continued as the K-II lights go on with force. I made my way into the living room and sat down on a chair while everyone else stayed where they had been during what is to this day known as the "tits in face incident."

"Can you come talk to me some more Emily? You remember how we communicate? Two lights for NO and three lights for YES, right?" Immediately, three lights turned on as we looked at each other in disbelief again.

"Have you spoken to any of us through the recorders we are carrying around?" Three lights.

"Cool, thank you! Was that you that just scared me at the foot of the stairs?" Three lights.

"Did you find that as funny as everyone else?" Two lights.

"I don't mind, Emily, I know you weren't trying to scare me. Is there someone or something here that wants to scare people?" Three strong lights.

"Alright, well, we are here to help Shane. You know Shane, right?" Three lights.

As the questions were asked, the lights would go out after a few seconds, but the timing of the lights coming on left me almost speechless. I had never dreamed that this type of communication was possible. This went on for several minutes. Yes; No; Yes; Yes to one question after another. We had seemed to determine that Emily was here as a protective force but was not allowed to leave. Her husband, whom she did not want to speak of for any length of time, was there as well but would likely not want to interact with us. There was also something else in the house, something she hesitated to communicate about for fear of repercussion.

If there was any truth to what we were seeing, we would have to find out if a woman named Emily died in this house, as we had been told this was true. Our first true lead in the case had been established. We needed to figure out what happened in the basement to bring such a negative energy and feeling to it, and we needed to find Emily's true identity. I had promised Emily I would do everything possible to help her find peace.

Emily all but begged us to stay out of the basement, but I explained that we could not do that. We were here to help Shane and find out what was going on down there and needed to do what we could to bring not only Shane, but this house, a sense of calm and peace. Shortly after this portion of the communication, Emily seemed to disappear. No more responses, not so much as two lights randomly coming on through the K-II, which in and of itself was incredible after what we had all just witnessed. Not once throughout the night did the lights come on unless we were in close proximity to some type of power source, which is very normal and expected. But sitting in two different rooms nowhere near any power source for a total of about twenty minutes having what seemed to be an intelligent conversation with someone—amazing. We simply could not believe what had just happened. You hear about these types of things, but until you are sitting in the room and experiencing it, you simply cannot wrap your brain around the impact this has on you. To this very day, I still can't wrap my brain around it.

It was getting on in the evening, and at this point, we were just past midnight. We knew Shane would be back eventually as he had requested to join us for a portion of the evening. I texted him and let him know we were ready for him to come back as things had seemed to calm in the house significantly after Emily seemed to disappear. We were very curious to see if the house felt any different when Shane was there after we had made what we thought to be pretty significant contact earlier in the evening. With Shane on the way, we all hung out on the front porch to prepare for him. We had decided we would spend time downstairs when he got home.

Shane's Arrival and Continuation of Investigation

Shane arrived and we decided to go back inside. Snort and Jason would hang out with Shane's girlfriend, Betty, in the main-floor living area while Jared and I accompanied Shane downstairs. Betty wanted to watch the DVR monitor, as there were a couple cameras set up in the basement, so she and Jason wanted to monitor that while Snort wandered throughout the upper level hoping to catch a glimpse of Emily or anything else lurking in the shadows.

Jared was manning the handheld camcorder as he went down the creaky stairs one at a time and was almost tripped by Toby as he stormed past us all and hit the basement floor. We all three hesitated as Toby began showing signs of agitation again as his vocalizations became more and more significant as we neared the bottom of the stairs. Shane reached the bottom of the stairs and picked Toby up in hopes of calming him down. This worked for a couple minutes as we made our way back behind the wall that stood about four feet high toward the back of the basement. Toby then wormed his way out of Shane's grasp and began walking around the three of us in circles as though he were herding us together like sheep. Jared took a few steps away from us because he wanted to get a better angle with the camera as Shane and I conducted our communication session. Toby got very irritated and followed Jared. He tried repeatedly to steer Jared back toward us as though he wanted to keep us all close together. We set up several pieces of equipment on the wall, including the K-II, the Mel-Meter and two mini Maglites.

"I want to communicate with whatever dark energy is down here. Come forward now and be heard," I said. There was no immediate response.

"Come forward now! I am not asking you; I am telling you! Get your ass out here and meet us face to face!" I continued, as Toby bolted faster than lightning up the stairs to the kitchen. Seemingly right as Toby reached the safety of the kitchen, the door to the basement closed with some force. Shane stood by me and simply watched the equipment on the wall as he could not hear what was going on.

"Dude, that freaking door just shut," I said to Jared and I radioed up to Jason and Snort to confirm that they were not moving around. They let me know they were not moving at all. We would see what really happened with the basement door later when we reviewed our camera footage. Toby never came anywhere close to it and unless an eight-pound cat carried the draft of a rather large engine, the door closed on its own—as though something was content with the fact that the obnoxious cat had gone and the three of us were still down inside its lair.

I communicated to Shane the basement door had just closed on its own and he began to get a little irritable. He had been completely quiet until shortly after I told him that.

Whispers of what sound like multiple voices began in close proximity to Shane and me through the voice recorder and quietly fade. [EVP]

"Turn this light on and show me what you are capable of, well, do it now!" I commanded. Almost immediately, both flashlights and all the lights on the K-II go on, and the Mel-Meter spiked from 0.0 to 3.5 mG and holds for a few seconds before all the lights went back off and the Mel-Meter read 0.0 mG. Shane reacted immediately and loudly. Since he had no idea how loud he was being, it frightened both Jared and me. I lightly touched his shoulder to try to calm him down. He settled down a little and I repeated my command: "Turn this light on and keep it on! Only one of them—I want to know how intelligent you are. Can you count to one?"

One of the flashlights came on as brightly as it possibly could and holds. I looked at Jared to confirm he was catching all this on camera and sure enough, he was.

"Turn the light back off. I am glad you are able to count to one," I said in a mocking tone as the light goes back off. Shane seemed to get very irritated almost immediately.

Whispers get louder and louder from seemingly multiple sources as Shane gets more and more irritated ... after about 15 seconds, the whispers are full on voices and Shane gets extremely frightened and begins yelling. [EVP]

At this point, I didn't know what was agitating Shane but I finally got him to calm down. When I reviewed this audio, I was frightened for him and had no doubts about his claims of being tormented by unseen forces. There is a theory that spirits communicate on a lower frequency than humans can often hear with their ears and at this point, I knew Shane could not hear anything, but if he were to hear something, it would be something on a much lower frequency than we can hear. He confirmed for me that while in the basement, he felt like he was being bothered by something. Could he hear and feel what I could only hear through my recording? There seemed to be something to this theory and I tried to look at this from his perspective. This is a man who lives in silence and has for his entire life, and to have that peaceful silence broken by something with the intention of tormenting and damaging him psychologically, I was angered for him and very worried about him.

I would text him between investigations after uncovering what had happened on the recorder to see if he recalled the incident I was wondering about. He knew exactly what I was talking about and explained that he felt like there were fingers touching him all over. He explained to me that it felt like fingernails were scratching at him on his face and neck, and he got really scared.

As we completed our time downstairs, we felt drained of all energy we once had and were ready to pack up for the night. Before I collected all the recorders, there was one still running near the master bedroom, which sat adjacent to the kitchen. As Shane went into the kitchen for a drink of water, there was a distinct message passed through the recorder that I would receive once we got home and I was able to review everything. This seemed to be a parting message for not only Shane, but for all of us as we wrap up our initial investigation.

"You're fucked." [EVP]

Review and Discussion from the First Investigation:

After we got back home to Kansas City, Snort and I hit the evidence review hard and came out knowing full well we had a very active and potentially dangerous case on our hands. The interaction with Emily showed us how much energy she possessed, which excited us, but it also indicated that whatever was downstairs may have even more energy because Emily seemed to shy away from contact when this dark energy was present. She would come and go at a moment's notice, and after reviewing everything, we felt certain that it was mainly because of this dark energy.

I contacted Shane to relay our findings and sent him a copy of the video file that very clearly showed that Toby was not within three feet of the basement door when it flew shut on its own. Nobody was in the vicinity when it happened and there was no moving air in the house. This was incredible, and it scared Shane, who said it was exactly like what had happened the day he was attacked by something that came up from the basement and threw the door open. I asked him when he would like us to come back and his response was simple, "As soon as possible, I need your help."

Everyone that was present during our initial investigation at Shane's house knew very well that this was not a typical case. Something was there and it had an agenda. We were quickly beginning to believe that it simply wanted anybody and everybody out—as though this house belonged to it. It certainly appeared very willing to do whatever was necessary to prove the point that everyone needed to simply get out. I was now determined to do whatever it took to help remove this force and bring Shane some peace in his home.

In the meantime, I needed to dig my heels in and find out anything and everything I could about this house and its seemingly dark past. I knew from experience that this particular area of Missouri had a reputation for being quite rough over the years and had allowed myself to be convinced nothing I might find out would shock me. I was wrong.

HISTORICAL RESEARCH
AND FINDINGS

"Wife of Local Mortician Remains Missing"

After an extensive manhunt for the wife of local mortician Emily Henderson, there are still no solid leads or any suggestion as to her whereabouts. Dr. Michael Henderson was unavailable for comment after being taken to the local police station and released after several hours.

—Excerpt from an article written in July, 1968

This was one of the first articles I came across when researching the address of Shane's house. I knew I needed to go through some of the local archives to learn about the history of the house and all its previous owners. This particular article was one of the first I found when digging into the archives of a local Mid-Missouri paper. The Henderson family lived in the house and Dr. Henderson ran his funeral parlor out of the exact same house. I could not believe what I was reading. It was as though the article found me.

This confirmed at least some of the local folklore about the house. After speaking to several locals who had been born and raised in the Mid-Missouri area, I learned that it had long been known as the haunted house on the block. When asked why, the vast majority responded with a story about some form of malpractice involving a local mortician. He was rumored to have mistreated the bodies of clients and had been rumored to bury empty coffins so he could keep the carcasses for his own personal research and amusement. In the end, the bodies were disposed of in a much more grisly manner. The locals were convinced he not only burned the bodies in the large furnace in the basement, but that he consumed parts of them before doing so. This was like something straight out of a horror movie. And now to find out his wife had gone missing and the case was still unsolved, I was floored.

I knew I had to contact the police and find out as much as possible. I ran into a wall with the police department very quickly when I explained what I was doing. As you may know, if you have ever done any research on a case, especially an open or unsolved case, they will supply only so much information. I was unable to find out much of anything other than what was already published through the library and was only able to conclude that Emily had never been found. It seemed as though she simply vanished one day, which led me to understand why so many rumors had been flying all over the community regarding what had happened to Mrs. Henderson so many years ago.

However, I was able to find an interesting article involving Dr. Michael Henderson that was published in 1974:

"Local Mortician Found Dead"

There has been no official word as to the cause of death, although it appears that Dr. Henderson took his own life inside his home. He suffered a gunshot wound to the head and his body was found after what appears to be an extended period of time postmortem.

Dr. Henderson had been rumored to have withdrawn from the public following the disappearance of his wife, Emily, over six years prior to his death. His death was officially ruled a suicide after the autopsy had been completed. At this point, the house was left abandoned for an extended time. It appeared that the Hendersons did not have any family interested in taking over the property, or what had become the family business. There did not appear to be an owner until it was purchased in 1982 by Shane's grandmother. She owned the house until her death in 1991.

The house had stayed in the family since Shane's grandmother purchased it. Many family members had lived in the house for periods of time, though no one stayed more than a couple years. This was something I needed to discuss with Shane and his mother.

Shane's mother reiterated the fact that no matter who had lived in the house over the years, they always experienced some strange activity. Everybody who had spent a significant amount of time in the house would report a wide range of activity. In many cases, they would hear people moving around freely in portions of the house that were empty. They would also report things being moved or disappearing regularly. Many people had felt as though they had been touched by something that was not there. One thing that really stood out was the fact that I had gathered enough information to show that many people who had spent a good period of time in the house were very prone to depression and lost the ability to function as they normally do. It seemed as though the house drained people of their energy and all positive feelings. The activity proved to be too much for everyone.

Shane moved in simply because he figured he would not be bothered by the things that went bump in the night because he could not hear them. Everyone who had stayed in the house for any extended period of time had experienced all sorts of sounds and had even seen objects moving. As is often the case, most people can take only so much of this type of activity before it becomes too much.

Not knowing when or what is going to happen and knowing something you cannot even see may do anything at any time is very unsettling, especially when you are in your own home.

For about a year and a half, Shane was relatively unbothered by the goings-on in the house. The activity seemed to pick up recently, and once it did, it escalated almost daily, and the occurrences seemed to be getting more and more brazen. Shane had had enough after being attacked by whatever lingers in the basement. Whatever it was, it definitely wanted to show that it was willing to come upstairs and meet him face to face in what appeared to be an attempt to remove him from the home permanently. I knew from my communications with Shane that it nearly had and may yet succeed. I recalled from my earlier conversation with Debbie that it was very likely whatever evil energy was enveloping this house may have been disturbed when they attempted to have the pastor cleanse the home. It was right around that time that things seemed to begin escalating out of control. It was becoming very apparent that whatever was here, was here to stay and would do whatever it needed to do to show anyone in the house that it was in charge.

Just a few nights before we were set to embark on our second investigation of Shane's home, I received a text message from him and he seemed panicked. His girlfriend, Betty, then called me so she could talk to me. I had asked Shane and Betty to clean the house from top to bottom before the next investigation. In many instances, the homes we investigate are simply overrun by pets or are cluttered with stuff that either gets in the way or could be considered potential dangers during a nighttime investigation. Shane and Betty were at the house cleaning when she called me.

"Brandon? Something is going on. Shane is freaking out," Betty told me when I answered the phone. I could hear Shane in the background, and he seemed very agitated.

"What is going on? Can you hear anything?" I asked.

"I heard a few thumping sounds upstairs and the cats are down here with us. We have been over here cleaning and—" Betty was interrupted by a loud yell from Shane, and as she screamed, the call was disconnected.

"Hello?! You there??" I asked, knowing the call had been disconnected. I immediately texted Shane and asked him to contact me as soon as possible. I then tried to call both Shane and Betty's numbers and there was no answer. At this point, I had no idea what just happened, but it did not sound good.

About five minutes later, my phone rings. It's Betty, so I answer quickly. "Are you guys okay??"

"No! He just took off! We were finishing up at the house and he started getting more and more freaked out, then there was a loud boom from upstairs and we could feel the floor shake. He was going up the stairs and a ball just flew down the stairs at him as though it was thrown and then he just took off. I'm still pissed!" Betty said, as I can hear Shane next to her still very excited.

"Okay, try to calm down. Are you guys still at the house?" I asked in an attempt to calm Betty down a little.

"Hell no! He ran out and I followed him. He says he's not going back there anymore," Betty said.

"Alright, we'll be there Friday. I will get there as early as I can. Will he at least go over there to let me in?"

"He said he will. What the hell is going on in there???"

"I don't know yet. I found some information that may prove useful, but in the meantime, does Shane have somewhere he can stay? I would recommend everyone stays out of the house for the time being." At this point I knew something was about to happen. I just didn't know what.

"Yeah, I'll put a key in the mailbox. Just let us know when you guys will be there, thanks," Betty said.

"No problem. See you Friday." I ended the call after they both seemed to have calmed down a little.

As I hung up my phone, I noticed I had received a text message from Jason.

"Dude, something is going on at Shane's, and it isn't good."

No shit, I thought to myself. I called Jason and explained what had just happened. I am again flabbergasted at his ability to pick these things up. He let me know that something not only wants Shane out of the house, but it wants everybody out. He was not going to be able to join us for the trip this time, so I figured it was time to call for a little backup.

Besides myself, Jared, and Snort, this time I would contact a good friend of mine to see if he and a couple of his team members wanted to join us.

"Hell yes, we'll be there! Sounds crazy!" Jeremiah said.

Jeremiah Norwood is a very good friend of mine, and at the time was the director of state operations for the Kansas State affiliation of Everyday Paranormal. They now operate under Everyday Legacy Paranormal and are a great group of people and investigators; I work with them as often as I can. Prior to this investigation, we had never worked with each other, but having many extensive conversations about this field of research, I knew we often saw eye to eye. He would bring his right and left hand team members, Claire and Ben Nichols, so we would have six investigators on site and ready for anything. Jeremiah had more investigative experience than I did, so I knew he and his team would be an asset.

For the upcoming investigation, our focus needed to be on making contact with Dr. and Mrs. Henderson as well as doing whatever it took to mingle with whatever, or whoever, was downstairs. At this point, I was very irritated with the fact that something could be so cowardly to attack someone as defenseless as Shane.

Whatever it was, if keeping people out of the house was its goal, it was getting closer and closer to it by the day. I was determined to make sure this did not happen.

There were still many unanswered questions, but I felt like we made some headway as to what direction we needed to take things. Was Dr. Henderson still in the house? I was not sure. For all I know, he may have been the upset entity that loomed in the basement. I was ready to get back down to that small Mid-Missouri town and do what I could to find out.

Because of the level of torment that seemed to be pointed in Shane's direction during the week following our visit, my patience was wearing thin very quickly. At this point, we had conducted one investigation and gathered a lot of data, but the reaction during the following days made me realize that we needed to go back as quickly as possible and get back to work.

The only downfall I had felt with selecting cases based on threat level rather than location was the fact that we typically found ourselves traveling a pretty good distance from Kansas City in order to conduct the investigation, which can be frustrating because we can't get to a client's house if we're needed at a moment's notice. However, being able to work on these cases meant more to me than accessibility. This was my promise to Shane and his family as well as every other family I have worked with over the years. I will do everything in my power to help you no matter how long it takes. If I work one case a year, or for multiple years, I don't care. Unfortunately, despite how it may look on television, if conducted properly, these cases take a very long time. You need to know what you are dealing with before you can find a solid and safe means of resolution. How can you possibly know what you are dealing with after one investigation? So I knew this would take time and I knew in my gut that something would happen. I simply did not know what it was. My only hope was that it did not have an adverse effect on the end result.

On the day we would head out for the second investigation, I got together with Jared and Snort and informed them about what had happened the other night with Shane and his girlfriend. They were not surprised as we had all developed a pretty sharp feeling of something very strange going on in the house. The fact that that entity was seemingly getting more brazen by the day did not shock us either, especially given the fact that Shane was present with only his girlfriend by his side. Whatever was going on, the being involved seemed happy to torment him, especially with nobody or just one person around. Hell, I recorded and listened to multiple voices seemingly taunting him right next to me and Jared during the previous investigation! I knew upon hearing that audio that this was a case that included something quite determined to obtain a goal of solitude within the home that had once belonged to the living. At this point, this being wanted this place to rot so it could have its own sanctuary without having to deal with the living. It seemed to mock the living as it pleased and without any fear of reprisal.

"Tonight," I explained to my crew, "I am going to get up close and personal with this thing. I don't know what is going to happen, but I need to turn its focus from Shane to me, and I can only see one way of doing that." They nodded in my direction, knowing what I meant without specifically saying it.

During the process of investigating someone's home, the last thing I would consider doing is using any type of provocation tactic. However, this case was different. The fact that whatever was in the house was so forward about tormenting Shane showed me that this thing did not care who may stand in front of it—it was willing to do whatever it took to make the person or persons leave. Having the thought of a disabled person being tormented by something so clever yet so transparent in his own home, in my mind, pissed me off to the point where I knew that I wanted to go face to face with it and see exactly what this thing was capable of.

Seven

INVESTIGATION #2

The three of us pulled up to the house as Shane arrived, but he did not want to get out of his truck. His girlfriend was with him and I asked for his permission to push a little harder tonight in hopes of prodding whatever was in the house to the point of interacting with me and the team on a more physical and personal level. I told him this would require more provocation and could end up pissing whatever it was off to the point where it might react negatively to anyone who went in the house for a while. He informed me that he would not be staying at the house anytime soon and gave me a key to his home. This was a first. I knew he and I had gained a pretty solid trust in the short time we had known each other, but handing me a key to his home was a gesture that meant the world to me. I would not let him down. Still, he barely knew us, so this level of trust was difficult to fathom. Was he really this desperate for help? Apparently desperate enough to give me the keys to his home in hopes I was capable of ridding him of this over-whelming nightmare. I was speechless. We gave each other a hug and he wished us luck. After I told him I would let him know when we were finished for the night, he and his girlfriend disappeared down the road.

Shortly after Shane had gone on his way, Jeremiah, Claire, and Ben pulled into the driveway. We all intro-duced ourselves to one another and quickly realized we were all in a pretty good spot. We all felt we were sur-rounded by a crew of very like-minded and capable people. I also knew I could learn a thing or two from them. Ben and Claire were a younger married couple and nice as could be. Jeremiah was an imposing figure. His bald head and burly frame standing about 6-foot-4 could be intimi-dating, but when he spoke in such an engaging manner, the fact that he looked like a "Hell's Angel" quickly sub-sided into him simply being a guy you were happy to be around. They all carried a very positive energy with them, and I gave them a status update regarding the case while Snort and Jared began setting up the camera equipment and running the cables. The most incredible thing about the people I work with is their inherent selflessness and ability to hit the ground running in any situation. Jared and Snort knew exactly where everything needed to be without any instruction or even being asked—they simply knew we had a limited time before we needed to get to work, so they hit it hard, and before I could blink, we were all set and the DVR was recording. We had six cameras running throughout the house as before and I delivered a digital voice recorder to each location and set up the audio so the investigation could begin at any time.

Jeremiah and his cohorts were certainly used to a certain way of doing business, but they had no problem allowing me to run the show, as it was our investigation and they were simply happy to lend a hand. These are the types of people that should be more prominent in this field of research. There was no bossing around, no finger-pointing, no turf wars or anything like that. It all simply fell into place. I suggested they set up any equipment they brought and enjoy the night. I told them I was planning on straying from our typical mode of operation by being a little more forceful tonight. After I had explained everything, they seemed to understand. I told them to feel free to get anything off their chest. Just before I broke everyone up to begin the investigation, I receive a text from Jason, who had to stay behind because he had a prior engagement: *"Watch your back! I don't even know why, but you guys should watch your backs; good luck."*

Well alright. I relayed the message to everyone just so they could all understand I wanted them to be "in the know" throughout the entire night. No surprises from an investigation standpoint. I wanted to make sure everyone had as much information possible. Sometimes Jason would have feelings about an investigation, whether he was there or not, that would turn out to be very relevant, so I wanted to make sure everyone was on guard and expecting the unexpected.

Jeremiah and Snort began the night in the basement, with Claire and Ben in the master bedroom on the main level while Jared and I worked our way upstairs to peek into the attic that we had not had a chance to explore yet. Jeremiah supplied me with a nice handheld camcorder, so I took it up with me as I climbed the ladder and went up into the wide-open attic space. There was very little walking room as most of the attic was insulation, as opposed to boards I trusted to hold my weight. I began my inquisition to anything that may linger in the darkness above the house.

Things seemed to be pretty quiet for the first twenty minutes or so, although as I sat in the attic, Jared got my attention, letting me know he heard a thumping sound coming from the room at the end of the hallway and was going to check it out. Snort contacted me via walkie-talkie and let me know they were feeling a cooling effect in the basement room, similar sounding to the experience Jared and I had during the previous investigation. Ben and Claire reported absolutely nothing out of the ordinary. Things were eerily quiet so far. I was not too surprised. Whatever was in this house seemed to be very cunning, and I anticipated it playing on all our nerves. One way to do that is to be completely silent, as though nothing at all is out of the ordinary. Talking up a case to someone, especially another team you are bringing in to assist for an investigation, is something I do carefully. Just because one night is seemingly out of control with the activity does not mean it will be the case every single time. They completely understood.

"Shhhh!!!" I heard suddenly coming from the bottom of the ladder I had climbed up to get to the attic.

"What?!" I asked down to Jared.

"Huh?" I heard from down the hall. Jared was in the room at the end of the hall checking the thumping noise from a couple minutes ago. He was nowhere near the area where I heard this shushing sound, so I hustled over to the attic's entryway and looked down. Nothing. Nobody was anywhere near the entry or the ladder.

I direct my questions in this manner: "Why are you telling me to be quiet? Do you realize why we are here tonight?" No response.

Jeremiah and Snort Session in the Basement Room

"Dude, it's freaking cold all of a sudden! Do you feel that?" Snort asked to make sure Jeremiah was feeling the same thing.

"No doubt, I'm showing 72.5. It was 79 just a minute ago," he told Snort as they powered on the Ghost Box in hopes of establishing early communication.

"Well, asshole, what do you have to say? Or are you scared of the two of us?" my brother began his line of questioning as only he can.

Jeremiah chuckled and almost immediately something responded from the Ghost Box. *"You're fucked ass."*

"Whoa! Did you hear that?! Ha!" Snort said as Jeremiah acknowledged.

"So we're fucked, huh? Maybe you're the one that is fucked and you just don't want to admit it. Could that be the case?" he pushed.

"Hahahaha," an almost inhuman voice laughed nearly in hysterics through the Box.

At this point, both Jeremiah and Snort realized something was going on and continued to pressure whatever it was to make contact in other ways than through the Ghost Box.

"Turn this light on, or are you too ignorant to figure out how to do that?" he said, pointing to his flashlight.

Suddenly, the flashlight holstered on Jeremiah's belt came on, and as they both noticed and reacted. Snort's flashlight that was setting on the windowsill came on too. Within seconds, two flashlights were turned on and they both reacted. "Damn! That was fast!" Jeremiah noted, as he says he felt like he was covered with a blast of cold.

Snort asked for the lights to be powered off at this time and his light went off, but Jeremiah's stayed on.

"Turn it off! I told you to turn them both off!" Snort pushed as Jeremiah's light turns off.

The odd thing about both of these lights turning on and off on their own, other than the simple fact that it happened, was that Snort's light was a mini Maglite that can be turned off and on by twisting the top of it. Jeremiah's light required clicking the bottom of it by pushing a soft rubber button. So two different lights requiring two different methods turned off and turned on upon request as they stood in what felt like a tomb as the chill to the air got thicker and thicker.

"Shit, my battery is dead on the recorder! That was quick!" Jeremiah said as he began to rustle through his pockets to get replacement batteries for his recorder, which had only been running for about twenty minutes.

Suddenly there was a series of loud noises that both Jeremiah and Snort could clearly hear. There was a loud POP followed quickly by a banging and then a loud thumping sound. The sounds came from the main area of the basement as they both paused and realized that things were getting a little hectic.

"Ahhh, dammit! What the hell?!" Jeremiah said all of a sudden with a startled annoyance to his tone.

"What?" Snort inquired.

"My back! All of a sudden, it went from being cold over here to hot and my back feels like it's on fire! The temp is showing 84 all of a sudden," he continues.

"Hahahaha . . . fuckers move!" the Ghost Box spits loudly.

"Um . . . buddy?" Snort called up to me on the walkie.

"Yes sir?" I responded as Jared made his way back down the hall toward me and as I began making my way down the ladder after an uneventful trip to the attic.

"Jeremiah has some big-ass scratches on his back, you need to see this. Bring a camera," Snort explained.

"Now we're talkin'," I said in an almost sarcastic tone.

"No bullshit; these are deep, shit is crazy down here," he said.

"On our way buddy." I got to the bottom of the ladder and Jared and I made our way to the bottom of the staircase.

"You guys doing okay in there?" I asked Ben and Claire.

"Yup, quiet so far."

I quickly explained why we were heading downstairs in a bit of a rush, and of course they make their way into the kitchen to follow us downstairs.

As we got to the bottom of the stairs, we all felt a strong cold breeze that seemed to zip right through us as we made our way to the room. Ben stopped on the stairs when he noticed it and quickly went back upstairs with Claire to see if they could figure out why a basement with no air circulation whatsoever could shoot such a strong chill up the steps. In my rush to get to the basement room with Jared, I barely stopped to even take note of the breeze despite it being quite noticeable.

"Dude, look at this!" Snort told me as I ready my camera.

Sure enough, as Jeremiah lifted the back of his shirt, there were two very pronounced scratches going all the way across the small of his back with a third one forming before our eyes. I began taking pictures from all angles and asked where he had been standing in the room when this happened. He explained the cold spot where he felt the drop in temperature, and without so much as moving four feet in any direction, the air was suddenly very warm as he felt the burning sensation on his back.

"Does it still hurt?" I asked him.

"It doesn't hurt so much as it just burns, like a sunburn," he said as I snap another picture.

By this time, Claire and Ben had made their way back down to us so they could check out the situation and they let me know they could not find a source of the breeze and it was nowhere to be found when they got back upstairs.

"White power!" A crystal clear and angry voice came through loud and clear from the Ghost Box, which had been running through the entire process.

"What?! So you are pissed off and racist? You like scratching people on the back, huh?" I began to mock whatever may be present while trying to keep my cool, as what just came through the Ghost Box was very intense and quite intimidating. What were we dealing with? Objects had been moved, people were attacked, and now we had physical markings on someone during the investigation. I also noted that whatever scratched Jeremiah, being the largest of all of us, might have been trying to make a point. Upon reviewing the audio after the investigation, I was shocked to find what had been recorded on my static recorder sitting in the room Jeremiah and Snort had been in. Just about a minute before Jeremiah feels the scratches on his back, there was a very clear and almost identical voice to the one we kept hearing in the Ghost Box that said: *"Get the big one."* [EVP]

At this point, we realized that whatever was here was not even the slightest bit worried or intimidated at our presence. In fact, it went after Jeremiah, who was by far the most physically imposing person involved thus far. So we had our work cut out for us.

To this point in the evening, we had been at it for a couple hours and despite starting slowly, the activity had picked up quickly and with reckless abandon. I did notice that we apparently had not had any contact whatsoever with the calming influence in the house that had been so eager to contact us during our first investigation. Where was Emily on this night? I decided to break with everyone and clear the house for a while to see if anything would go on while we were out of the house.

We made our way out of the house one by one and decided to come back in a half hour after things calmed down a little. I did not know it at the time, but was stunned to find out that things not only did not calm down during our break, but they picked up drastically.

In an instant, the house came to life with a barrage of incredibly loud noises that could be heard throughout the house. To start it off, a trio of echoing blasts rang from the large furnace in the basement, as though someone had punched it repeatedly. The bangs were followed immediately by the sound of footsteps creaking on the basement stairs as though someone was walking up or down them at a normal pace. The floor to the kitchen area above begins to creak as though someone was walking just upstairs from where the recorder sat. As the sound of the stairs creaking continued, there was a large crashing sound from the kitchen as though a plate or something had been thrown to the ground. This crash was simultaneously accompanied by a crashing sound in the main area of the basement that resembled the sound of a board being thrown to the ground. Sounds throughout the house were being recorded at a rapid pace for several minutes without any break. It was total chaos. Suddenly the sound of bootsteps came from the main hallway and kitchen as well as what sounded like something heavy being dragged across the floor. After a few more seconds, the heavy steps and the dragging sound transferred from up in the main hallway and kitchen area to the main area of the basement, as though something was brought down to the basement level without paying attention to the laws of physics. After almost four straight minutes of the house sounding as though it was completely alive, all the sounds just stopped—all at once. Right as the sounds ended, a muffled chuckling sound came from just inside the dungeon room. Then the house was silent.

The sounds of this house literally coming to life began just after we closed the front door behind us as we began our break and continued with an almost arrogant and emphatic personality of their own for almost four straight minutes before the house suddenly became completely silent. Just after the silence fell, there were whispers from all over the house that showed up on four different audio recorders. The words being whispered were inaudible, but clearly there. There were more voices than we could count. As I reviewed the audio and discovered what had been captured, I was not entirely convinced this house was not actually alive. I had never heard or experienced anything like it before.

Eight

SIDE EFFECTS

I had conducted dozens of investigations and had helped several families deal with and find conclusions to unexplained issues in their homes. We had successfully cleansed homes and given people common-sense answers to what they had built up as being devastating circumstances. But it was not until we had taken on Shane's case that I felt like my work was affecting my daily life. The dreams were becoming more and more real almost every single night and I found myself fighting to keep from jumping to any conclusions about the case. I was positive something in the house was doing everything it could to make its presence known not only during our investigations, but now it seemed to be creeping into our personal lives. I could not tell if it was a show of power or if my mind was blowing the situation out of proportion. The dreams had become an obstacle and I was determined to face them just as I was determined to face anything in order to offer Shane some kind of help. I wanted him to be able to rest peacefully at night, and if it cost me a bit of my personal comfort, I had made the decision to accept that as a hazard of the job.

When you deal with nightmares on a regular basis for a long time, like I have with the Nemesis, you simply adapt as best you can within your daily life. It becomes part of you. By the time I began investigating Shane's home, I had become used to the dreams. Over the course of time following investigations at Shane's house, the dreams became more vivid and threatening. At times while I was reviewing all the data we had collected, I knew something was sending a very clear message. A part of me said I should be taking these messages more seriously. I wasn't sure at the time. I was positive these were mind games and I was simply determined to push through and stay the course. I considered it this dark energy's way of throwing me off course in hopes I'd lose sight of my end goal—to see Shane and anyone else that lived in that house live peacefully and without worry.

As the investigations at Shane's mounted, the dreams became more frequent. I kept noticing the little things around me change. My demeanor, my energy level, and of course my ability to sleep soundly all changed for the worse. I could feel a physical difference in myself. Everyone in my everyday life noticed the differences as well; they would just make little comments like "Are you okay?" My answer was simply that I was just not sleeping well, but was otherwise fine. With every fiber of my being, I wanted to deny what was going on. This case was gripping me as hard as it could and it had become the most important thing in my life. In my eyes, this was not necessarily a bad thing, although it was. As you will come to find out, allowing a case to take on a life of its own and hold your life hostage should not be an option. I keep referring back to my calling in life, which I used to justify the changes in my life and simply chalked it up to experiencing some side effects of the job. This rationalization is the same as a football player who might develop frequent headaches over the course of time. He has taken one hit to the head after another—it stands to reason that he will have headaches. Well, I put my mind and body on the line within every single investigation. Literally daring whatever lay in wait to do whatever it needed to do, physical or otherwise, to me to prove its very existence. What should I have expected other than unexplained occurrences and an overall effect on my dreams? As the case developed, I grew as a person. I knew this case would make me a much better investigator in the future. And when Shane could sleep soundly through the night in his home, after whatever darkness that lurked in his home's corners and nooks burned in the Hell from which it came, I would proudly hold my head high knowing that my ability to adapt to the changes and overcome these obstacles made it possible. This would not be the first case I came out on top in, and in my mind at the time, it would certainly not be the last. I would simply do the militaristic thing and adapt and overcome any obstacles set before me.

The problem with these latest dreams was not only the disturbing things that happened in them—the pain and torture of the souls involved—but the fact that the Nemesis was there all the time, even if it was just him in the background. He smiled. He was also accompanied by the man that had shown up years earlier and had been his trusty sidekick ever since. The thing about these dreams is they became more and more personal. One night it would involve my kids and their safety, the next it would be my parents, and so on. These were not just simple dreams of people I love being in trouble, they seemed to include tortured souls. These dreams gave me a gut feeling that my family was at risk. It took me longer and longer to recover after every single investigation. Without fail, things got worse the more I went to Shane's house. The problem was I had given him my word that I would not stop until I had answers. That remained the top priority. So I pressed on.

As I went to sleep just a few nights before the next scheduled trip to Shane's house, there was a noticeable difference in the air—something thick, something simply out of place. Because I had to wake up early for work, I knew I had to go to sleep one way or the other, although it was not the first thing on my "things I want to do" list. In many ways, I felt like I was in the middle of a Nightmare on Elm Street film. I knew what waited for me and I knew I had to face it, so I did.

A dark and damp place surrounds me. I can hear distant cries and screams; they are muffled. I can distinctly hear the dripping of water, or something. There is a crunch beneath my feet with every step I take. I don't even want to know what this crunch is, but a faint light allows me to see that they are whatever is left of some type of bones. I am in a pit of bones and every step becomes more and more difficult to accomplish. The screams, the moans, and the cries remain distant, but distinct. I don't even know what my objective is; there is no immediate physical threat to me, but knowing my surroundings are those of rotting corpses, I know I need to get out of this place.

A familiar laugh rings into this room that I can't escape and at first, it is muffled. It gets louder and more clear by the minute. I know this laugh. It comes from prior dreams stemming from years of nightmares. I know it's the Nemesis. He is close by. This doesn't bother me as much as it probably should because he has never been of any threat to me, but before I can even get my bearings, there he is—the sidekick. He is there simply staring at me. He has a grin on his face, an expression that never changes. He simply hates me. Some people use the word "hate" freely, I do not. There is nothing but pure hatred in the sidekick's eyes. He wants me dead and he wants it soon. I try harder to maneuver my way through the crunch of the bones beneath my feet. I am crawling toward the sound of the screams and cries, they are no longer so distant. As I turn a corner, I see a dark figure and as quickly as I see the details of its figure, it is gone. The laughing stops as I immediately understand that my children are in danger. They are struggling for their lives and I am helpless; I can't maneuver my body through the mountain of bones. Every single step takes every ounce of energy I have, and it seems the closer I get to progressing toward where I need to be, the room seems to move or grow. I can't reach them. I am completely helpless.

A steady stream of cold sweat runs down my face. I can feel my shirt soaked with the same ice cold sweat as I come to and realize again, my nightmares have bested me. My breath is short and at a pace that would make someone think I just finished running a half marathon. I rub my eyes and wipe away the tears, trying to convince my mind that it was just a dream. This has happened a thousand times before; why can't I handle this any better than I do?! I lay back in my bed and I feel so drained that getting up to take a shower and prepare for work seems like an impossible task. I lay there looking at my clock. It is 5:16. My alarm isn't supposed to go off until 6:05. There I am, in my bed, breathing like I just finished a very difficult workout and covered in sweat. I simply stare at my clock and know there are many options, but going back to sleep is not one of them. I turn on my TV and find something to watch for the next hour and gather myself enough to get into the shower and get ready for another day. This is my life; this is what I do. How much of this is to be blamed on my decisions and how much should be blamed on my life experiences? An impossible question to answer, but one that I ask myself almost daily.

Nine

THE MILL

With everything going on at Shane's house, I knew we would not be able to make the trip to Mid-Missouri every single weekend. We'd now made three trips in five weeks, but I also wanted to start looking for other potential locations to check out on our spare time.

As an investigator, I am always seeking out new ways to anticipate where unexplained activity may take place. Whether there is a reason geographically or otherwise, I find it extremely important to research common themes in many types of locations because that may provide insight as to why certain activity happens in different places. I have always had an endless fascination for places that are considered to be "Ghost Towns," so I have done extensive research on the numerous places that qualify as Ghost

Towns. There are a million reasons why a place could have gone from boom to bust. Natural disasters, dried-up resources, and many other things could have caused older establishments to become abandoned. These locations are spread out all over the world and sometimes a story that goes along with the location is just too good to pass up. That was the case with a location in Cameron, Missouri. A Ghost Town called Haun's Mill. The story alone will make your skin crawl, so I naturally wanted to look into it. Although I could find no reports of paranormal activity, the story told me that there was a good chance I may find out differently if I investigated the location.

Despite being heavily involved with Shane's case, I can't help but look for new ideas. My true passion is writing and the thought of making independent films, so I keep a constant lookout for potential locations that could lead to an incredible story. If done right, I believe these stories not only bring to light forgotten history of our country, but they also educate people and allow them to learn how to better open their hearts and minds and look at the world from a fresh perspective. With the media beating us over the head with politics and sensational news, I feel like we as a society have forgotten what a fascinating and beautiful world we live in.

I came across a story that took place on October 30, 1838. It is a story of madness and gross discrimination that led to the massacre of nineteen innocent men, women, and children and thirteen additional nonfatal injuries. Only three of the Missouri Militiamen involved in the attack were injured, and none were killed at the scene. During this time period, discrimination against religions deemed different was an epidemic, typically leading to false allegations of witchcraft and things involving the devil. This was the case with the Mormon people who had established communities in Missouri.

Gov. Lilburn Boggs sent down an "Extermination Order," however, many believed that the militia involved in the massacre could not have received any such orders because of the difficulty spreading orders and word quickly at this time. This militia took it upon themselves to attack the community at Haun's Mill and brutally murdered innocent people and ended up disposing of many of the bodies in a nearby (and now mysteriously difficult to find) well. They threw dirt and straw over the remains and left this community burning and broken behind all in the name of hatred.

After reading this heart-wrenching story, I knew I had to investigate this location. I felt that many innocent souls may have been trapped at this location considering the fear and other disturbing circumstances. I wanted to investigate to see if there was anything remaining from so many years before. I knew there could also be a dark energy present, but my concern was releasing any innocent souls that might be stuck in a type of hell because of how they had met their ultimate demise.

Jared and I set out on a scouting trip on a hot September day and had no idea what to expect. From my research, I knew there were a couple Indian burial grounds nearby, but had no idea what to expect regarding the layout of what was left of Haun's Mill. There were no standing structures, only a memorial on the banks of Shoal Creek. As we ventured down a dirt road miles from civilization, we began to get deeper and deeper into the middle of nowhere and the roads became more and more impassable as we drove. Being that I was driving my KIA Optima, I knew I was getting very close to hitting the limit of my road trip warrior of a vehicle as the standing water and mud became higher and thicker as I drove deeper into the depths of northern Missouri. We finally hit a point in the road where we knew we could drive no further, so we found a place to back the KIA in and set out on foot during the hot, late-afternoon hours. We headed down the muddy dirt road toward the predetermined coordinates leading us to the final resting place of so many innocent people.

We had walked about a mile when we began to approach a turn in the road and could see what appeared to be some type of sign, likely the memorial we had been searching for. As we saw the sign in the distance, my K-II meter began going off madly. We were literally miles from anywhere. There were no visible man-made power sources for miles that could be causing the device to function this way. The lights lit up without being prompted and Jared immediately pointed the camera at the meter so he could document what was happening. Suddenly, a burst of cold sliced through the hot and humid air, and we felt like we were in the presence of something very different. We did not want to jump to conclusions, but I immediately began recording on one of my digital recorders to try and capture anything that might have been attempting to communicate with us. The K-II meter does not just go off for no reason—it requires some type of atmospheric change and normally involves some type of energy source. It is very typical for a K-II meter to go off while near electronic devices such as microwaves or refrigerators, but we were miles from any such source. So the lights going off like crazy were very notable. We continued our trek toward the sign and sure enough, we had found the memorial. It was very obvious that it had been some time since anyone had done much to maintain the area. Everything was overgrown, from the large field that sprawled for well over a hundred yards off the side of the walking path we had discovered to the vegetation that had grown over the memorial. This place had been truly abandoned and forgotten about.

Jared and I decided to explore using the map I had printed, which gave us an idea as to how the establishment of Haun's Mill would have been set up back when it was the home of the Mormon community. We walked along the banks of Shoal Creek and kept getting off-and-on hits on the K-II meter. We soon felt the need to try to make sense of the reaction, so we began to request the lights to come on as we commanded. Sure enough, we were immediately able to get the device to illuminate a certain number of lights as we requested them. While it was still too early to assume we were in the presence of a spirit, from the communication we were receiving, it seemed as though we were in the presence of a child. I would eventually review the audio from my recorder, which seemed to solidify this as the truth.

Immediately after asking if someone was there, I received a childlike response that very clearly said *"Help us."* [EVP]. The voice was soft and high-pitched. Jared and I were miles from any other living soul and this voice was very clearly not one of ours. I was unsure if this was a residual plea or one of intelligence and possibly a poor lost soul looking for peace.

As the sun began to set, the overall feel of the location turned very dark very fast. Almost immediately Jared and I could hear the distinct howls of a pack of coyotes. Birds were everywhere, and it was obvious we were in the middle of nowhere and nature had taken over this location—what was once a thriving community had all but been erased. We continued to get off-and-on hits with the K-II meter, and I had taken the time to review several of the recordings before we decided what to do next. The childlike EVP was not the only foreign voice I had captured in the few short hours we had been exploring this beautiful, remote location. It was by far the clearest though. As night fell over us, the feeling of the area went almost immediately from serene to very overwhelming and intimidating. A heaviness to the air was very apparent and felt like we could cut through it with a knife.

Upon review of one of the audio sessions, I came across another, very different voice that was much more clear than the mumbled voices that would require closer review on the computer. I had simply asked who is present and there was an immediate response: *"Go away! Angry."* [EVP]. We had been told to leave and apparently whatever wanted us to leave also wanted us to know how it felt about us being there in the first place. At the time, we were in the middle of nowhere completely surrounded by pitch blackness and all the sounds of nature. It was a little disturbing and we were both getting a little edgy.

We decided to go back to the memorial and venture down the trail behind it so we could get a closer look at the creek. We had heard noises coming from that direction and sure enough, as soon as we settled in and established our communication point, standing about twenty feet above the creek, we could hear what sounded like distinct footsteps along the shoreline, along with the trickle of the water. The footsteps shuffled in areas surrounding the creek where leaves had begun to fall, and the subtle splash of footsteps seemed to be walking in the shallow waters of the creek. We examined the entire area using our flashlights, but we saw nobody, nothing. Once we turned the lights off, we almost immediately both saw different movements in the woods that were illuminated by nothing but the moonlight. It was a beautiful and spooky feeling, but we both kept seeing what looked like shadows moving in and out of the trees along the banks of the creek. At this point, we were rattled—what had begun as a scouting trip had quickly turned into a pretty dire situation. We were over a mile from our vehicle and surrounded by nothing but nature with little to no cell phone reception. It seemed as the seconds ticked by, the energy of this place closed in on us. It felt dark and very intimidating. Around midnight, we decided to head back to the car and call our scouting trip a success. This location would definitely be worth a full-on investigation in the very near future. So we began to make our way back to the car and walked down the remote road that was covered with standing water and mud.

As we worked our way back down the road, we kept hearing sounds coming from the thick brush that surrounded us and could not tell if we were being stalked by something physical or something else. We knew there were coyotes and had also seen deer, so we knew that any number of wild animals could have been surrounding us. At this point, I held tightly onto my machete I had brought and we quickened our pace heading back to the car. The K-II lights began to go off again, and we had felt very stressed because of the complete unknown we were surrounded by. Finally, we approached the car, and we could both not get in fast enough. The obstacles that still lay ahead had not even crossed my mind to this point. We were barely able to get the car parked in the one dry location we could find for miles during the daylight, now we would have to navigate these treacherous roads in pitch blackness, which would prove to be damn near impossible.

"Dude, this is going to suck," Jared proclaimed.

"Agreed." I immediately confirmed his fears.

As we headed out on the roads, my immediate concern was navigating the puddles—not just going around them, but figuring out which ones were passable. It was a maze of large truck tires that had beaten their way into the dirt road, creating a seemingly impassable obstacle course for a car as small as mine. I had barely a foot of ground clearance and I knew the vast majority of these holes extended much deeper than that. In these types of areas, cars simply do not travel on these roads; everyone who lives here has a large truck; if they don't, they simply stay away from these roads. My thoughts earlier were that the roads would be passable because of the memorial. I thought they would be kept up enough for vehicles to come and go so people could come and pay their respects. I couldn't have been more wrong.

As I aggressively approached the standing water trying to build momentum, we slid through a first and then a second standing body of mud. We had traveled about fifty yards and it felt like ten miles. As much as I tried to maintain our forward momentum, it was impossible because I had to continuously choose which side of the road to try to navigate. We approached a no-win situation with the next portion of the road—nothing but standing water. This was the location we almost got stuck in during our trip in earlier. So I hit the gas and hoped to God that we get through and sure enough, immediately, we were going nowhere and there was nothing underneath me but spinning tires. I tried to reverse and back up in hopes we would get another shot, but the KIA was not going anywhere. We weren't going to move forward or back. I simply looked at Jared...

"Well buddy, we're screwed."

"Dammit, no options," Jared said as he opened his door. I noticed the water is barely an inch below his door, it was almost pouring into the car as he takes a step out of the car and is immediately knee deep in muddy water. "Son of a bitch!" Jared began to put all his weight into the door and tried everything to give us the slightest momentum and we slowly move forward. After about ten exhausting minutes, we somehow negotiate our way out of this hole. The only problem with that was about twenty feet in front of us was another one that looked identical to the one that just tried to swallow the KIA whole.

"Follow me dude," Jared said as he splashes mud and water all over the place as he slowly walked toward the next mud hole. I was simply going to follow him out at this point. We have about a half mile of this slop to work our way through and the only feasible way was for me to follow him as he nuts up and walks through all the obstacles in front of us. He did not know if he was walking through a snake pit or what the hell else may be lurking, but we did not have a choice.

After about forty-five minutes, we finally hit the dirt road, it was rough, but it was dry. Jared got back in the car covered from head to toe in shit and he simply looks at me "What the hell bro!"

"Unreal buddy, some freaking scouting trip, huh???" I tried to lighten the mood a little.

At this point, there was absolutely nothing either of us could do but be thankful we made it out in one piece and simply label it the cluster that it was. We had a car in one piece and despite being a little shaken and ridiculously covered in slop, we made it out. We were on our way home and it was about 1:30 in the morning. By the time I dropped Jared off at home, we were both completely exhausted, so we packed it in and decided we would have to look into another approach when we went back the next time.

After getting some rest, I was able to really take in the entire situation and realized we had stumbled across an amazing location that had been completely forgotten about by our society. This saddened me, but it also gave me a great sense of pride because we did our research and on nothing more than a gut feeling and ended up coming across a seemingly very active location. We would be able to work this place for some time to come and try to figure out exactly what was going on at this beautiful place.

We would go back many times within the next month leading up to the anniversary date of the massacre that had taken place well over a century ago and it would prove to be a location that provided us with much insight into what was actually there. This place was amazing.

Ten

MEETINGS

As the investigation of Shane's home went on, I felt more and more that I needed to reach out to certain local people for advice as well as strength. I grew up going to Catholic schools and have made it no secret that I have had some personal issues with many aspects of organized religion as a whole, not just Catholicism. However, to this very day, I have never once wavered in my love and belief in the power of God. I grew up with certain teachings and hold many of them dear to my heart. I decided it was time to reach back out to my roots and hold onto a faith because in the end, we are all after the same thing—helping those in need regardless of the cost. I had certain expectations as I began to make phone calls and set up meetings. I did not want to get my hopes too high because I was well aware of the Church's stance on this sort of research. My hope was to find someone with experience and an open mind willing to accept what I do for what it is; my fear was I would run into walls.

It did not take me long to schedule an appointment at Catholic Church headquarters in downtown Kansas City. Little else was discussed during my initial phone conversation with Monsignor Ryan because I felt the details were best discussed in person. I wanted to get the vibe as to whether or not the Monsignor was willing to assist me or not.

"Good afternoon, Brandon, how may I be of assistance?" the Monsignor said as I entered his office. He was a soft-spoken man with a very calm demeanor. I decided I would not waste any time beating around the bush.

"Monsignor Ryan, I appreciate your time and do not want to waste it. I work with people who have issues in their homes regarding unexplained activity that can sometimes become hostile. My main focus is attempting to help people who are afraid of their homes to find peace. I have been successful in the past and am asking you if you can refer me to someone who has experience dealing with this sort of problem so that I may get advice as needed, possibly assistance of some sort as needed as well." I explained this in a matter-of-fact tone and simply looked into his eyes. His eyes went from open to almost fierce.

"Brandon, you must understand the Catholic Church has a certain stance on these sort of things. What exactly

are you referring to when you say 'unexplained activity'?"
he asked.

"Demons. Dark energy that has the ability to oppress
people when they are subjected to it long enough. Anything that may make people living somewhere live in fear
for whatever reason. There is no exact word to use to describe it. What I do is try to make people sleep better at
night and try to rid them of problems." I could see where
the conversation was going.

"Brandon, I cannot get into specifics on this subject. I
have very little experience working with this type of problem. It sounds like a spiritual issue. What do you want to
get out of this?" The tone of the conversation took a turn I
was hoping to avoid.

"I ask nothing in return. My passions lie in filmmak-
ing and writing. I want to help people that deal with real
evil on a daily basis. I want to educate people and show
them there are people that live in fear and they don't have
to. I want to do my part in putting to rest certain miscon-
ceptions about paranormal activity." I gave the Monsignor
a general overview of my intentions.

"Have you ever thought about becoming a man of the
cloth, Brandon?" the Monsignor asked me frankly. "These
types of issues can only be handled by a true man of God."

"I have thought about becoming a man of the cloth
before, but determined that it was not my calling. I simply
want to be able to put my passions toward helping those
in need. I don't believe having an official title as a priest is

required for this," I tried to explain, as I knew I had just run into my first wall. I needed to be a priest in order to get anyone to communicate with me.

"Brandon, I am going to give you the phone number of a gentleman I know that has worked with these types of issues for a very long time. I do not know what he will tell you, but I do believe your intentions are pure. He may not tell you everything you want to know and he may not be able to help you at all, but I am happy to give you his number. I will pray for your well-being and hope you find what you need." The Monsignor clearly wanted to end the conversation.

"Thank you for your help. I appreciate you taking the time to see me. I will call the Deacon and hope he can point me in the right direction." I shook the Monsignor's hand and he embraced me and gave me an almost fearful look into my eyes before I head out of his office.

I had a phone call to make.

After a very brief phone call with Deacon Freddy, I agreed to meet him north of the river near a church in a historic area of Kansas City that had once been known to house many gangsters. The neighborhood now leaves a lot to be desired, it is broken down on many levels and has become an area known as one to stay away from. The architecture in the area left visual reminders of what a beautiful and well-developed area it used to be. Time has not been kind to many areas in Kansas City, and this neighborhood was a poster child of how time is not always friendly to our society. There was an endless amount of history surrounding this area, but these days, it simply seemed to desperately cry out for help.

I wander around this beautiful church awaiting the arrival of Deacon Freddy, who had told me to meet him behind the church so we could talk. I made my way to the rear entrance and noticed a very worn out minivan pull up just outside the parking lot. With the engine still running a gentleman took a step out of the minivan and waved to me to come over toward him. Being unsure as to whether this was the man I was waiting on, I pointed to myself in a way to ask him if he was looking for me and he reiterated his motioning for me to come toward him. I approached the van and the man said, "Get in" without any emotion; it was a simple request.

I approached the old van and climbed into the passenger side and noticed a very cluttered vehicle as Deacon Freddy and I made brief introductions to one another as we shook hands. Freddy was dressed just like it was another day, he had a jacket and long pants on as he shifted in the driver's seat to try to get himself comfortable. He seemed to be a nice enough person based on first impressions, but also had a very clear look to his face that told me clearly we were not here to beat around the bush.

"Monsignor Ryan gave me a brief description of what you were speaking with him about and he informed me he referred you to me," Freddy began.

"Right, he said you have a lot of experience in dealing with situations involving people having problems in their homes," I began to explain as he cut me off.

"I deal with spiritual warfare, Brandon. I have performed more exorcisms than I can count over the years, and I believe you should not be seeking out any dark energies without being a man of the cloth. You may encounter true evil, and you do not have the ability to protect yourself or others unless you become a deacon or a priest," Freddy said firmly. He was a very blunt person. On many levels, I could appreciate this.

"Freddy, I feel like I have received a true calling to do what I do. I also realize there may be times I could use advice or help as well," I explained as Freddy cut me off again.

"You may have good intentions, but you have to understand, I can't tell you certain things because I don't believe you have the right to ask certain questions. At this point, I don't know whether you were sent to me by God or by Satan," Freddy said, as I got frustrated.

How dare this man sit there and tell me what information I was "worthy" of?! I should not have been surprised, but in a big way, I was. I was disappointed. I was hoping Freddy would take me seriously and be able to set aside the recruitment long enough to tell me whether he believed he could help me. It seemed that because I was not a man of the cloth, he was not allowed to take me seriously.

"Understand the position I am in, Brandon. I see the Devil work every day and I have seen evil claim more souls than I can count. I have someone approach me expressing interest in involving himself in situations that deal with pure evil. You cannot ask for a more dangerous situation, and I have been taught that you need certain protection and training in order to deal with these forces," Freddy began to explain.

"Freddy, I have had personal issues with the church for a very long time. I have never for a second lost my faith in God, but I could never commit myself and my life to a specific religion that says I need certain training in order to help people. I can't accept that as the only option." Freddy did not cut me off, so I continued.

"For a very long time, I have felt like I have been called to work on these types of cases and have been able to help people. Why can I not develop my skills and help people without having some formal title with an organized religion? To my knowledge there are many Saints in the Catholic church that never held formal positions in the church, why would the church take such a hard-line stance that blocks so many people with such good intentions from being able to help people?"

"Brandon, I don't know how much help I will be to you, you really should look into praying. I can help you get into certain areas of the church that will help you develop your spirituality and eventually show you what you need to know. You will be able to help people in the way you claim you want to help them. It will take a large commitment from you though." Freddy emphasized the necessity that I attend formal training and start looking into ways I could become a man of the cloth.

Our conversation went on for quite a long time. We ended up sitting in the worn-out minivan for more than two hours. I explained my stance on the church and we discussed the human side as well as the spiritual side of things, but in the end, I felt I was left hanging. I felt like I was given an ultimatum, which was my biggest fear. Of course, had I visited a Jew, a Baptist, a Lutheran, or anyone else stemming from any other organized religion, I would have still been told that I needed to be some sort of preacher or priest or deacon. I was very disappointed. I had truly hoped humanity would reign supreme and they would focus on my desire to help good people.

I do believe there is a certain level of spirituality that needs to be held dearly throughout the investigations I conduct and I always make sure I go into any situation with respect and faith in the power of good. Evil exists, so there must also be the power of Good. I have worked with clients from all different religious backgrounds because they wanted my help. And I don't believe their religious affiliation is ever the cause of the problems in their homes.

I felt as I left the meeting with Freddy that I had been told there is only one way I can follow the path I have been called to follow. It would require me dedicating my life to prayer and obtaining an official title in the church. Despite bracing myself for this outcome, I felt very let down. Ideally, I wanted this conversation to simply focus on the victims, not the status of those of us looking to find solutions.

I walked away from my meetings with these two obviously good men knowing I was on my own. I was on my own in a physical sense, but again, I never for a second lost sight of the fact that I have God by my side. I do not preach, I do not judge anyone based on their religious beliefs, and I do not have the arrogance to decide how others should approach their own spirituality. I simply confirm what I already know in my heart. I cannot bring organized religion into my investigations. I simply need to know that I am protected by a higher power and my faith in good will never waver. I will research any and every method to help those in need. Will I ever have to come face to face with evil? I believe it is inevitable, and all I can do is carry the strength and faith in the powers that be to know I will be able to face anything that stands in front of me and threatens the lives of innocent people involved in these situations.

Eleven

SCIENCE

In the field of paranormal research, fighting the natural tendency to become disheartened in the face of most people questioning the legitimacy of what we do is a constant battle. This type of research definitely differs from natural sciences such as chemistry and physics. From the very beginning of my investigative career, I had thought about the importance of incorporating truly scientific methods of research and including science-minded people into the investigations. I was fortunate enough to come across a brilliant and thankfully open-minded individual through a job I had. He had an overwhelming number of qualifications that nobody could deny when it came to his view on any type of unexplained activity. I knew I had asked him about joining us at Shane's home. I wanted to get his unbiased take on all the activity. So Jason and I sat down with Dr. Richard Joseph and discussed the idea of him joining us that upcoming weekend on an investigation (our first in two weeks) and he was surprisingly very excited about it. Dr. Joseph had earned his PhD in particle physics from a very well-known and prestigious university.

I explained to Dr. Joseph that he was there to observe and I would simply like his feedback as everything is going on from his scientific perspective. I also explained that I wanted to conduct a widely known, but very controversial experiment. I had never conducted this experiment before, but having Dr. Joseph present was an opportunity to have a fresh, scientific persective on the situation, which would allow us to properly evaluate the outcome. I knew this experiment had many risks, but at this point, Shane had been chased from his home and I wanted to step outside the box and try to figure out exactly what was present and if there was any chance of getting rid of it. Although I had already concluded that whatever was there was a very intelligent and powerful force, I still could not specifically identify it.

What is known as the Ganzfeld Experiment is a very controversial experiment that has been conducted by psychologists since Wolfgang Metzger devised it in the 1930s. The theory is when the subject is deprived of certain senses, they may be able to pick up on other energies surrounding them. I will refrain from providing certain details as I do not recommend anyone tries it, especially in a location that may house dark energy because the consequences can be very frightening and dangerous.

The basics of the experiment require the subject to be still in a location where their senses of hearing and sight are taken away—they are only hearing white noise while being still in complete darkness with their eyes covered. This theoretically opens the subject up to experience sounds and feelings that are inwardly generated and can open the person up to whatever unseen energy may be lingering. The results of this experiment over the course of time have varied greatly. One of the experiment's original main goals was to prove the existing capability of people to develop and use telepathic skills. Normally when used in this type of environment, the goal is not necessarily to prove telepathic tendencies, but to open the subject up to communication and physical vulnerability to whatever may be present. This is dangerous because the subject may be opened up to physical or psychological injury and possibly even possession. I decided I would attempt the experiment at Shane's during our next investigation to see just what this force was capable of.

This weekend, we would bring Dr. Joseph with us and all four of us, Jared, Snort, Jason, and I were able to go as well. I was excited to have everyone involved and felt like this had potential to be the most productive investigation since the case began. I explained to Shane that it would probably be a good idea for him to keep his distance from the house before and after the investigation, as I did not know what we might do in regard to stirring up activity. He reiterated that he would never go in the house again unless it was to move out. He welcomed us to try any experiments we felt could make an impact so we set the wheels in motion to conduct a very advanced and risky experiment during the coming weekend. This is when I believe the investigation became "real" and the wheels were set in motion to change my way of looking at the paranormal permanently.

The week leading up to the investigation, I had been very busy trying to get organized and make sure the experiment and the overall investigation would go off without a hitch. A certain level of stress came with conducting the investigation because I knew there would be some type of outcome. Nothing in me thought for a second that this upcoming weekend would not have long-term affects. I was absolutely right.

As the week progressed, my ability to sleep soundly dissipated. I was having almost constant nightmares. I found myself trapped in the abyss of bones more and more often. The once distant mocking laughter was now so close I could almost feel the breath as it came from the darkness. It was the same laughter I had caught several times through our audio devices during the prior investigations. Sometimes it was embedded in the background of whatever was going on; sometimes it was as though whatever was laughing was doing so at point blank range into the recorder. Either way, it was ever present and it was more and more intimidating considering it rang through like an echo in my mind at all times, especially while I was sleeping. The man in my dreams had become a regular occurrence. When I was growing up, seeing him in my dreams was a rarity, but lately, it was constant. I could always see him and his smug grin and in the shadows behind him was the other person. The other person had began showing up shortly following my stint in the military. I knew why he was there and I wondered if he would ever go away. It seemed he and the man in my dreams came hand in hand at this point and had no intention of going anywhere anytime soon.

As the dreams seemed to intensify, so did the vividness of these two sinister men. I was feeling drained all day and could not fall asleep at night; I felt like I was a character in a *Nightmare on Elm Street* movie. Needing to sleep, not wanting to sleep, knowing before it even happened what is going to happen. It began to take its toll on my psyche. I decided to sit down with Jason and have a conversation about the upcoming weekend.

"Shoot me straight. You know what I want to do and you know why I want to do it, right?" I asked him.

"Yes, and I am on record saying that this is very risky and have already felt that something negative will come out of it as a result," Jason told me very candidly. "Obviously I cannot say for sure what will happen, but I am positive there will be repercussions."

"I understand. Shane is out of the house permanently and we have an opportunity to do this experiment and see if there is any way it can help us communicate with it and see how we can get rid of this thing. Do you think it can help?" I asked.

"I think it may clarify some things, but in the end, we are opening doors that we may not be able to shut. You are inviting whatever it is to invade your space and it will," he told me in his typical Jason *"warning, you are crazy"* tone.

Our conversation continued for a few more minutes and in the end, we both concluded that it was worth the risk to conduct the experiment. I guess I made a good argument—he went from being adamantly against the experiment to being reluctantly supportive. I understand I more or less twisted his arm and was simply grateful he agreed to be present in order to provide support. I understood his hesitation and told him I would in no way hold it against him if he wanted to bow out of the experiment, but he would be there out of loyalty. He believes that I am in this for the right reasons, so he understands my need to push the envelope on occasion.

The plan to conduct the Ganzfeld Experment was in place. I had all the details down and, while apprehensive, I was convinced this procedure could lead us to establish a more solid foundation as to who or what was infesting Shane's house. I was ready for this and was ecstatic that Dr. Joseph would be joining us to witness everything. The idea of having a true scientist with us was incredible. More than anything, I wanted to see what he saw and was endlessly curious to hear his explanation for some of the activity we had been regularly experiencing in the house. If he had a legitimate and common-sense explanation for different types of activity, I was completely on board. This would allow us to document everything from an unbiased perspective, which I wholeheartedly believe brings legitimacy to what we do and allows for true progress in this field of research.

The Investigation

Jared, Jason, Snort, and I packed up all our equipment and hit the road. We picked Dr. Joseph up along the way and he really seemed to be looking forward to the experience. What separated him from most scientists I have come across in dealing with the unknown is that he kept an open mind about everything. He was looking to understand what was possible. I believe he had many questions and wanted to partake in this investigation so he could start to put together his own theories. Science tells us that something is not real if it cannot be repeated. I believe this is one of the largest hurdles we have to overcome in finding true progress in finding answers.

In this world, there are millions of incidents that are classified as "paranormal" and at its core, that simply means an occurrence that cannot be explained with conventional teachings that have been put together over thousands of years. In such a large existence, I often find it curious that we have such a difficult time stepping outside the normal box when it comes to our thoughts on what is possible. Tonight I felt like we would make some progress in our own studies that would allow us to take a small step toward establishing the ability to mix science with spirituality. My hope was that something big and noticeable would happen and be documented so we could all put our heads together and analyze whatever it was without preconceived notions.

As we drove to Shane's house, the sun was setting. We got a little later start than normal because we had to work around Dr. Joseph's schedule. As we were driving, I had been texting back and forth with Shane and he made it clear that he would not be there this evening. He welcomed us to stay as long as we would like, but earlier in the week while he and his girlfriend had been at the house cleaning up, he nearly lost consciousness and felt very ill. As soon as he left the house he felt perfectly fine, but he decided he did not want anything to do with the investigation tonight. That was probably for the best because I knew that this experiment could cause things to escalate. The last thing I wanted to do was to involve him in anything that may cause the activity in the house to gain strength. I would in essence be daring whatever was in the house to give me all it has to give. I wanted to know just how powerful this energy was.

Dr. Joseph had many questions for us as we traveled. I answered them as best I could because I wanted him to have as much information as possible so he could understand what to be on guard for. In the end, I explained to Dr. Joseph that he should expect the unexpected. I had no idea what would happen during this experiment, but from my research, I understood that the presence of the energy is asked to become closely involved with the person doing the experiment. The idea is to block off the senses of sound and sight to allow whatever is there to interact with the person on a spiritual level. In a way, it is an open invitation for the energy to do whatever it wants to do and has been said to open spiritual doorways and have long-term effects on the person involved, who is quite vulnerable in this scenario. I knew there was a level of naivete in my desire to conduct this experiment, but I also knew that I would never grow as an investigator if I was not willing to go out on a limb. In my mind, I was doing what needed to be done and I felt comfortable with any results because I had Jason and Dr. Joseph there. Jason has always given me confidence when it comes to dealing with energy of any kind. He has many years of experience dealing with the paranormal. Having Dr. Joseph there gave me the confidence that someone without preconceived notions would be present and would keep an open mind and try to find reasonable explanations without jumping to conclusions. In short, I was very confident this was the right situation to conduct this experiment.

We arrived at Shane's house and were greeted as usual by Tommy as he stood upon his perch on the front steps. He was very welcoming and vocal as we got to work setting up the equipment once we let ourselves into the house. Toby was also inside, and he was oddly calm tonight. Normally he would get excited when we all showed up and he would rub against our legs and be an entertaining nuisance as we set everything up for the investigation. Tonight, however, he was a little different. He seemed almost drugged, which was strange. As Jared and Snort started running cable to set up the cameras, Jason and I gave Dr. Joseph a tour of the house so he'd get familiar with the place. He did admit that there was a pretty ominous feeling to the air inside the house. Jason had quickly become short of breath several times as we were walking throughout the house. I ended up sending Jason outside to help Jared and Snort get everything together and make sure we were able to start the investigation as soon as possible. Because the air felt very odd on this particular evening, I immediately began running a recorder. I almost always start a recorder as soon as we begin setting up the equipment, because it seems quite common that odd things happen at the most inopportune times. At Shane's, it was not uncommon to hear all kinds of voices as I reviewed the audio data following the investigation. It seemed to range from the almost constant mumbling voices seeming to have conversations to blatant threats that were much more audible. It simply seemed like this house had some sort of spiritual infestation. It did not matter if it was upstairs, on the main floor, or the basement, there just seemed to be an incredible amount of ever-present energy and activity. Tonight was no different.

Before every investigation, I remind everyone involved to make sure they do or say whatever they need to do in order to protect themselves from whatever we may encounter. I typically carry a few small stones and a St. Michael medallion to protect myself. After the investigations, I go home and cleanse the stones, which are theoretically capable of capturing and blocking dark energies. Thus far it was a tried-and-true method of protection. I have never implemented a specific prayer or process for everyone because we all have our own beliefs, backgrounds, and ways of protecting ourselves.

Upon review of the audio that had been running on the main level of the house while we were setting up the equipment, as Jared walked by responding to a question Snort had asked him from upstairs, there was an interruption: *"Don't do it"* rang through the recorder clear as day. The thing that made this stand out so much was the fact that the voice was clearly a female. The issue was that there was not a female anywhere near the house. It never ceases to amaze me when these things happen. How is it possible to hear a female voice speaking as loudly as any of us and without a female present? It is just one of the many things that makes my hair stand on end every time I hear something similar during the data review. This voice seemed to be pleading with us, but it would not be heard until it was well past the time the warning could be taken into consideration.

Before long, all the equipment was set up, and we were ready to start the investigation. We all made comments about how strange the air felt that evening. The house was always stuffy and had a strange feeling, and the smell was never what any of us would consider "normal." Sometimes it was difficult to breathe, and we had to chalk that up to the fact that no matter how much cleaning had been done, the cat pretty much ran the household and had left his mark to the point where this house would probably never smell "normal" again.

As we began the investigation, I took Dr. Joseph to the dungeon in the basement to start off in hopes that we could get something going quickly. The other fellas were scattered throughout the house, and we decided to start off by simply sitting quietly for about ten minutes, no questions, no anything. Just sitting silently to see if anything was going on. Sure enough, it was not long before we all started hearing things. Snort reported hearing creaking sounds in the hallway on the top floor, although it did not stand out as something outrageous, it seemed more like an old house settling as they are prone to do. Jared and Jason had started in the kitchen on the main level, and they both felt several cold drafts. They did not hear anything out of the ordinary.

Suddenly, a series of footsteps came from nowhere. The footsteps were so pronounced that Snort assumed it was one of us walking around.

There was one step after another. Snort heard it, then another, and another.

"Buddy?" Snort gently called into the hallway.

No answer.

"You out there?" He continued to try to get the attention of whoever was walking up the stairs in his direction; there was no response.

"Hey fellas, are any of you moving? Walking up and down the steps?" Snort called out on the radio, breaking the deafening silence that hung throughout the house.

Jared and Jason simply looked at each other. They had assumed the steps they were hearing coming from the main stairway in the entrance area was Snort coming downstairs to check on them. Snort was sitting silently upstairs in the nursery.

Dr. Joseph and I looked at each other and confirmed we were sitting silently in the dungeon.

"No, buddy, nobody is moving. What did you hear?" I called over the radio.

"Someone coming up the stairs in the hallway," he confirmed.

"We heard it too. We thought it was Snort coming downstairs," Jason confirmed.

Suddenly, a loud booming sound came from the main area of the basement.

Dr. Joseph and I were startled to hear something banging on the water heater in the main area of the basement. It was immediately followed by what sounded like something being dragged across the floor. We quickly jumped up and headed to the main area of the basement.

"What the hell was that?!" Jason called over the radio.

"Come on downstairs, fellas," I said. "Snort, go ahead and stay upstairs and check out what is going on around the stairs." I asked for Jared and Jason to come downstairs so we could be in two places at once. I wanted Snort to stay upstairs because this was not the first time we had heard clear steps being taken that were not our own.

Jason and Jared slowly made their way down the creaky stairs and joined Dr. Joseph and me in the basement. I tell them to set up shop behind the wall in the back of the basement while we got set up in the dungeon.

"Mine; Go now!!!" [EVP]

After reviewing the audio, I found a clear-as-day EVP that seemed to be telling us to get the hell out of the house. We did not need to hear the EVP to know that. It was clear just by the feel to the air. It was just a matter of how it would decide to try to get rid of us. Everyone's hearts were pumping pretty good at this point.

Dr. Joseph and I settled back in the dungeon and almost immediately got interaction with the K-II meter. As we began asking questions, the lights were going ballistic, although not with any rhyme or reason. The reaction of the lights did not feel as cooperative as we had experienced many times before. This time it just seemed like something was making clear its stance that it wanted us to leave. Dr. Joseph got closer to the K-II to try to see if anything in

particular may be causing the reaction. It was simply sitting still on the windowsill as we were trying to get a reaction. As Dr. Joseph inspected the meter, there was the sudden sound of glass hitting the floor within a few feet of us.

As I looked down, one of the candles that had been
set up in the corner of the room was rolling toward me.
Neither of us were within five feet of the candle and
we were standing on a concrete floor. There was no air
movement in the house, let alone in the dungeon room.
We also felt no vibrations on the floor or anything. The
candles had been standing on solid, level ground and all
of a sudden, one of them was rolling across the floor in
our direction. Dr. Joseph looked at me.

"Did you kick that?" he asked.

"No, I am standing still. Do you feel that?" I asked
him to see if he was also feeling the sudden presence of
what feels like electricity in the air.

"The static?" Dr. Joseph inquired.

"Yeah, it feels like there is a buzz to the air. It wasn't
here a minute ago," I pointed out to him.

"What happened???" Jared asked from the main area
of the basement.

I explained to both Jared and Jason what had happened, and they were both a little flustered. I called up to
Snort to see if anything else was going on upstairs, and he
confirmed all was quiet. I told him to make his way toward
us in the basement. The evening started off quickly, and I
was able to confirm later upon reviewing our audio that

there were many threatening voices surrounding us. Some were familiar and others seemed to be voices we had not heard before. The EVPs were littered with profanity, and we were told several times to leave. It was pretty typical that we collected these kind of threats within our audio devices. At this point I wanted to get something visual on our cameras. Everything seemed very subtle, and most of the data we were collecting that stood out seemed to be in the form of audio that we could not hear at the time it was recorded.

Snort joined us in the basement, and he was breathing heavily as he got to the bottom of the stairs as though he had been rushing toward us.

"Buddy, I don't know what just happened, but right when I was at the top of the stairs, I felt like something bum rushed me and I got shoved toward the stairs!" he told us as we all looked at one another and wondered what may happen next. This was the first time since the night Jeremiah and his team joined us that everything felt very up front and in our face, as though it was trying to get us out of the house as quickly as possible.

All of a sudden there was a very distinct and obvious grumbling sound, almost as though someone's stomach was loudly objecting to its digestive process. This was followed by what sounded like a rabid dog growling.

We all heard these sounds coming from the top of the stairs, and then we heard a creaking as though the door was slowly shutting at the top of the stairs. I worked my way over there and sure enough, the door had been completely open and was now about halfway closed. Suddenly I feel like something rushed toward me, and I jumped back, startled. "Holy shit!"

"What the hell dude?!" my brother asked as I stood at the foot of the stairs. Things were happening fast and furious tonight and I began to wonder if these were all signs that conducting the experiment later in the evening would be a mistake. But I was determined to perform this experiment. I needed to see what happened.

We all stood quietly in the basement and were almost able to read each other's minds as we simply wondered what was next. I looked at Dr. Joseph, who seemed flustered. Although he kept his cool, it was very noticeable that he was taking note of everything happening.

"Well?" I looked at Dr. Joseph trying to coax a reaction.

"I don't know; I don't know what is going on. This is crazy," the doctor says in a very calm voice, although his voice was obviously shaky.

I decided we needed to step outside for a few minutes to get ourselves together. Before we left, we made sure we had cameras on all the areas of interest and had audio set up with the cameras. I wanted to see if all this activity continued when we were outside. It did.

"Hahahaha Fucker." [EVP]

While reviewing the audio from the recorder that had been placed at the bottom of the basement stairs, right where I felt like I was rushed, this ominous laugh came through very clearly only about a minute after we had vacated the area. The mumbling voices were prominent all over the house, and they were almost constant as well. The thought of these mumbling voices not being audible as we listened was getting more and more spooky as they happened. Knowing you are constantly surrounded by voices you cannot hear definitely takes a toll and makes you understand that it is very common to feel these energy sources even though you may not be able to see or hear them. You can feel them, and I was quickly learning that listening to my instinct and my body was very important. The natural tendency is to dismiss or ignore these feelings, but this house was teaching me a lesson. Always listen to your instincts. Our minds and bodies are much more perceptive than we give them credit for. Remember, we are taught from a very early age that these things are a figment of our imaginations. I was finding out firsthand that that is not always the case.

We were all outside monitoring the DVR system waiting for something to stand out, but nothing jumped out at us. Snort and I were having a cigarette and taking a quick walk around the house discussing what we had experienced and the plan was for the rest of the night. Jared called to us over the radio, "Dude, you need to see this!"

Snort and I hustled back to the crew to see what had Jared up in arms. He had the camera that was set up downstairs paused and a look on his face like he had, pardon the pun, seen a ghost.

"Check this shit out. Just watch and let me know what you see," Jared said as he hit play.

"Whoa!" Snort and I exclaim at the same time after watching about ten seconds of the video.

"Holy shit! That was ridiculous!" I was stunned at what I had just seen. The camera was standing on a concrete ledge at the bottom of the basement stairs and pointed at an angle so we could see all the way up the stairs, the entire staircase, and a good portion of the main area of the basement. We watched as the night shot of the camera had everything very well illuminated and then a black mass made its way down the stairs. It did not seem like it was at all concerned, it was simply making its way to the bottom of the stairs and all of a sudden, after about three solid seconds of watching this mass come down the stairs, the camera angle got adjusted. The angle was quickly turned from pointing up the stairs to the left, so the stairs were no longer visible, only the main area of the basement remained in frame.

We were all pretty amazed at what we had just seen. It was obviously time to get back into the house. I wanted to conduct the Ganzfeld Experiment as soon as possible. So we got our shit together and headed back inside. As we walked back into the house, a slam came from the kitchen area, so I quickly headed toward it and sure enough, the basement door was closed. Within a few seconds, Jared came inside and walked up to me as I was standing at the door and he just looked at me.

"Dude, what is going on? I just watched that door shut," he said to me as I smiled and realized that we were getting exactly what we asked for on this incredible night.

The Ganzfeld Experiment

We set the chair up in the dungeon as I prepared everything for the experiment. We had the red light set up as well. The idea is to open the person involved up to whatever may be residing in the area. The sense of sight is blocked by placing half ping-pong balls over the eyes and taped to the face and headphones are placed over the subject that will stream white noise. This allows the subject to remain undistracted by the surroundings and goings on in the room. The theory is whatever energy may be present can easily interact with the subject through the white noise of the headphones; it can physically interact as well. The long-standing theory is that spirits can communicate more easily through white noise because it takes less energy than producing audible sounds that people can hear with their own ears. My intent was to allow the energy to interact with me on an audible and physical level without being distracted by other noises and words made by anyone present. Jared and Dr. Joseph would be in the room while I conducted the experiment. Jason and Snort would be outside the dungeon room in the main area of the basement to monitor anything of note going on outside the room.

Dr. Joseph would simply observe the experiment and anything strange that may happen while I was in the trance state, and Jared was the equipment technician, so I wanted him there just in case anything malfunctioned. He has also always been a little jumpy, so I thought it would be a good test for him to have an up-close-and-personal experience. I always told everyone on my team that I would always test them because I believe it very important for everyone to face their fears and allow these investigations to get them out of their comfort zones—it gives them a chance to really experience things that may make them think. Of course, if they refuse to be in a position, I never force them; everyone should have the right to stand down if they are too uncomfortable. In this case, Jared was very interested in having an up-close-and-personal seat for the experiment.

Jason and Snort were both a little standoffish with the whole experiment. I took their concerns into account, but decided I needed to do this. They both understood, but they still felt the need to warn me.

As I took my place in the chair that we had set up, I began to get the equipment set up; the room had audio running in every corner, as did every level of the house. The second I sat down in the chair to prepare to start the experiment, the flashlight I had placed on the windowsill of the dungeon came on with vigor. Just a few seconds before the light came, I'd asked if there was any type of message I needed before I performed the experiment. I looked at Dr.

Joseph, who was standing just behind me, and his face was flush. All the color in his face seemed to instantly disappear as I saw him stare at the light. He had confirmed the light was completely off, and the only way it could come on was to twist the top of the flashlight well over a quarter turn.

"Holy shit," Dr. Joseph said in a hesitant and calm voice.

"Are you trying to tell me I shouldn't conduct this experiment?" I asked as I settled into the chair. Immediately the K-II lights went ballistic as the flashlight turned off.

I told Dr. Joseph to check the flashlight before we proceeded with the experiment, and he let me know the light was extremely cold to the touch. The room was a warm 77 degrees, so there was really no reason the light would feel as though we just pulled it out of a freezer, but it did. As he handed it to me so I could confirm how cold it was, it came on again simultaneously with the K-II lights going all the way on. The K-II has five lights on it, as each one is lit up it indicates a higher level of electromagnetic energy that is being detected. It is not common for all the lights to come on unless you hold it very close to some type of electrical appliance such as a microwave or refrigerator. There was no power in this room whatsoever, so the fact that in a period of about a minute all the lights had been illuminated so strongly was very notable. Jason and Snort came into the dungeon room for a minute to confirm what had been happening, and the second they came into the room, there was a loud shuffling sound in the main area of the basement. Jared was very close to the door that led into the dungeon, so he looked out through the windows of the door that separated us from the main area of the basement and the dank dungeon and jumped back quickly as though he was very startled.

"Oh God! What the hell???!!!" Jared exclaimed as he quickly moved away from the door.

"What?!" I asked him.

"Dude, I shit you not. I just saw a shadow and then a face in the window of the door!" Jared told me. I can see the hesitation and concern all over everyone's face.

"Alright, let's chill out. I want to get this started," I used the calmest voice I could muster. Inside I was rattled. I had no idea what was about to happen, but everything going on during the setup seemed to be trying to tell me this was a bad idea. So of course I proceeded.

"Are you sure?" Jason asked me before he and Snort headed back out into the basement.

"Yeah, screw it, let's do this," I tell him as they headed back out into the basement where there seemed to be something lurking. I told them to conduct their own experiments while we did ours. I simply asked them to keep the volume down.

I sat back in the chair as Jared placed the headphones over my ears, and I made sure I had three recorders running as he placed the ping-pong balls over my eyes. He turned on the red lamp; it was only a few feet away from my face, so all I could see was a red glow as the white noise came screaming through the headphones. I could not see or hear anything else. It was time to start the experiment.

For the first couple minutes, I simply sat in silence to observe anything I may feel or hear through the white noise. I had informed Jared and Dr. Joseph I needed them to stay as still and quiet as possible so I would not misconstrue their movement or voices as something else. I had told them I would be in this state for forty minutes. The first ten minutes I would simply sit quietly; the last thirty minutes I would try to verbally interact with anything that may be present.

Not long after it started, I heard a very distinct laughing sound coming through the headphones. It was the same ominous laughing sound I had heard many times while reviewing audio data from our previous investigations. Several times we'd thought we had heard laughing in the house with our own ears as well, so this did not come as a surprise. I remained silent after verbally marking what I had heard.

Several more minutes passed as I sat quietly. Suddenly I felt something brush against my left arm and almost immediately saw the red glow interrupted by a bright light. It was the flashlight on the windowsill to my left. The flashlight came on and I noted I felt something brush against my arm. I had asked Jared to touch me if he was the one that had brushed my arm. He did not respond.

As I continued to try to focus on what was going on within the white noise, Dr. Joseph picked up the flashlight and turned it off. I had asked him to remove it from the equation because at this point, if the energy present was going to manipulate anything, I wanted it to manipulate what had been set up for the experiment.

I began to hear a growling sound and what sounded like a female voice, although I could not understand what had been said. At this point, I felt pretty uncomfortable because it seemed like something was lurking, but it was not coming forth in a direct way to communicate.

The remainder of the first ten minutes passed and I began to slowly try to interact with whatever might be present. I asked simple questions.

"Did you touch me? If so, can you do it again?" I asked, with no response.

"Was that you laughing? What is so funny? You seem to laugh a lot but you never actually do anything." I spoke in a sarcastic tone, daring whatever might be there to come toward me and prove me wrong. I still got no response.

All of a sudden, I hear a childlike voice come clearly through the white noise, *"Can you help???"*

"You need help? If so, I need you to cooperate with me. Can you please turn the lights on by touching the device in my hand?" I asked as Jared gently touched my foot to indicate the K-II lights came on just after I asked them to. I was holding the device in my hand and had let Jared know I needed him to give me a subtle indicator when something happens, especially after I asked it to.

"So you need help?" I continued as the lights go out on the K-II. "Are you afraid? Is there something else here with you?"

Suddenly through the white noise there is a scream—as if someone was screaming for their life. This startled me badly and suddenly I felt something large bump into the chair I was sitting in. At this point, I was very rattled and I asked Jared to let me know if either he or Dr. Joseph had bumped the chair; no response.

I continued as best I could with the experiment as Jared had not indicated that the forty minutes were up, although, at this point in all honesty, I was finished. I was extremely uncomfortable and did not know what to expect next. Unbeknownst to me, Jason and Snort made their way into the dungeon to observe the last ten minutes of the experiment. They quietly entered the room and the door to the dungeon room creaked slowly behind them as though it was closing on its own. Everyone took note of it as the slow creak was very creepy. I was unaware of this at the time as I continued to ask occasional questions. I was not feeling like I was getting a lot of real-time interaction and was simply ready for the next several minutes to pass.

With about a minute left in the experiment, I made a last push to see if I could coax something to happen.

"Whatever dark energy is here, I need to know who and what you are. Quit being a chump and step forward.

I need you to show me what you are capable of." I received an immediate response through the white noise.

"Fuck you; die!" the raspy words bark through as though it was someone sitting right next to me speaking in a normal tone right in my ear.

I immediately take the headphones off and try to quickly take the ping-pong balls off my eyes. That was it. I was finished. At the time, everyone knew something happened, but they did not know what it was.

"What happened?!" Jared asked.

"I don't know, I'm done," I lied to him because I wanted to go back and review the recording before I told any of them what I believe was said. They all knew something big happened because I had responded so quickly after demanding some action.

In some ways the experiment was a success; in others, I knew it was something I probably should not have done. From the second I regained my senses, I felt different. To this day, I find it hard to describe, but I felt different. Something had changed and I could not tell if it was physically or mentally, or something in between. It felt as though I had come upon and had some type of energy in me that was not there before. I am in no way trying to say something entered me because I do not really believe that is what happened. I am simply saying there was something extra that had not been there before, that was there now. It worried me, but at the same time, I decided we needed to continue with the investigation.

We took a break outside the house to allow everyone to calm down a little and we all took turns telling each other what our own experiences were during the experiment. I told everyone everything, except what I heard at the very end. It concerned me because it was a direct response to my provocation and the words were very clear. I do not typically recommend anyone go overboard with provoking anything in someone's home. I had a lot of experience with this type of investigating and I knew we had a good chance at coaxing a reaction, so I took calculated risks knowing we had the ability to calm things down if they got stirred up too much. I never provoke anything in a person's home without their consent and I had been given the green light to do whatever necessary to get a reaction. We had received all kinds of threats from scary-sounding voices on many investigations, including at Shane's house. This one was different because it immediately reminded me of the clear words I had heard a few years earlier, just before my friend R.J.'s death.

"Get you dead!" These were the words from our very first investigation at Snort's house that rang in my mind as clearly as though I had heard them yesterday. It was not the same voice, but it was clear, and it was frightening. I let it go for the night and decided we would finish the investigation, and I would then take the chance to re-evaluate the situation with Shane's house. I was beginning to think something very dangerous was going on. Maybe it sounds like I had been sleepwalking through

my previous investigations and taking all the activity and threats too lightly, but when we work on cases like this, threats and activity are very common. This particular case was simply developing a different demeanor than it had at the very beginning. There had been many signs that should have tipped us off, but we pressed on and were determined one way or another we would help Shane.

During our break, we had discussed having someone else conduct the same experiment. We decided that we would try it again, but we would stay out of the basement. Snort would conduct the experiment in the living room, where we seemed to get a lot of interaction from Emily. Jason would then conduct the experiment in Shane's room so we could see if anything happened, knowing he is very sensitive.

Each experiment was conducted for about twenty minutes, and nothing out of the ordinary seemed to happen. Both Snort and Jason thought they may have heard something here and there, but nothing definitive seemed to come through. The one thing that my brother noticed while performing the experiment was that he said he saw what seemed to be a shadowy type figure that hovered over him while he lay on the couch. He could not make out an exact shape, but the fact that he saw this where he did, it was definitely notable. Because a light is pointed at the subject wearing the ping-pong balls over their eyes during the experiment, it was fascinating that he could see something changing the glowing tone that had been consistent throughout the experiment. Not a lot of audio or anything came out of either experiment, but Snort said that is what he saw, and we noted that nobody was moving in any way when he claimed to have seen it.

We still had a couple more hours left, and I wanted to get our money's worth while Dr. Joseph was present. I knew we might not get a chance to have him with us again, so we decided to make one last push in the basement to see if we could make something else significant happen. At this point in the night, my energy was completely drained. I felt like I had run a marathon, so I would be happy when the night finally came to an end. I did feel like it had been a very productive night, so I wanted to finish it on a strong note.

We all went back down to the basement and we decide to finish off what was already a very eventful night by seeing if we can convince something else to happen. We would not be disappointed.

As we started to get set up in the basement, something odd happened. On a quick side note, we had been working on a case prior to Shane's case that had taken us up to Omaha, Nebraska, and I had noted something that happened before we investigated. While we were in the basement at this other house, Jared had this sudden need to take a dump. As he put it, this was not just any dump. Have you ever been driving during rush hour and that familiar feeling hits and before you know it, you are pinching your butt shut as tightly as you possibly can so you don't destroy your car and whatever you are wearing? You end up breaking into cold sweats and pray to everything holy that you can make it to a toilet in time to deposit whatever is about to explode from inside you? Well, we all got a kick out of watching Jared break into these familiar cold sweats as he stood with his ass pointed toward the opened screen door in the basement as our client took us through the house and told us stories about activity that had been going on. Jared was very obviously in misery and in a way we felt bad for enjoying it as much as we did, but we are human and funny is funny. This was funny. Not thirty seconds after the client finished the tour and left the house, Jared sprinted, well, hustled as quickly as possible to the bathroom and proceeded to make his much-needed deposit. Jared has told me that he never has these issues on a normal basis, and it was notable that it only seemed to happen when we were in the middle of a location that turned out to be very active and oftentimes surrounded by very obvious negative energy.

As we got everything set up to finish off the night in the basement, suddenly Jared had a familiar look come over his face.

"Dude, I gotta go!" Jared says with a look of utter devastation on his face.

We all immediately began to giggle.

"Do what you gotta do, buddy. We will just get started," I told Jared, trying to keep a straight face.

"I don't want to go up there by myself! This place is crazy!" Jared says as we all lose our ability to stay serious. We pretty much all hit the ground crying with laughter as he sprinted up the stairs.

"I got your back, buddy, right behind you," Jason said in a half-comforting and half-hysterical voice. He followed Jared up the stairs laughing hysterically.

As the audio recorders are placing such hilarity into our permanent files, something different than anything I have ever heard in my life happened.

"Alright buddy, go ahead and head into the dungeon," I told Snort, as he and Dr. Joseph made their way into the dungeon room.

"I don't want to play; it's just a game." [EVP]

None of us heard anything at the time, but as I reviewed the audio from this ridiculous chain of events, this was the exact same childlike voice I had heard earlier through the white noise during the Ganzfeld Experiment. This voice was the clearest thing I had ever heard that none of us actually heard with our own ears. The words rang through the recorder clear as a bell. I could not believe it. I was also able to confirm it was in fact the same voice.

Once Jared and Jason joined us after his near catastrophe, we continued the investigation, but we found it difficult to keep everything on a serious note because of Jared. We were able to keep it together long enough to finish off the investigation with another hour or so in the basement. We were actually able to get the flashlights to cooperate with us for a period of about ten minutes during that time as well. Dr. Joseph was floored every time it happened, he simply could not understand how this was possible. At one point, I had lined up two flashlights on the wall in the main basement area and we were able to establish communication with both flashlights. We asked a series of yes-or-no questions and depending on which light came on, we were hoping we had established the energy's ability to give us answers. We were able to document the entire thing with the camera, so it was a great way to end the evening.

"Come to me." [EVP]

I was startled to hear what was said right next to me in the basement just before we decided to begin packing up. I didn't hear this command until I reviewed the audio within the few days following our trip to Shane's house, but it rang loud and clear and seemed to be directed at me. The voice was all too familiar—it was the raspy voice that sounded very threatening and had become a regular source of many threatening EVPs that we had captured during our investigations. Because I had conducted the Ganzfeld Experiment on this night, it made me pause. I wondered if I had done something I shouldn't have, but at the same time, I felt like it had been an extremely productive night.

Dr. Joseph thanked us for taking him as we dropped him off at his vehicle a few hours after the investigation. It had been a very long and eventful night. I had texted Shane and let him know when we left and that we had locked up the house. He thanked us for coming down. As I got home just before sunrise, I still couldn't shake this feeling. It was this different, heavy feeling. I chalked it up to being exhausted, and decided I would upload everything to the computer and try to get some sleep.

Twelve

POST GANZFELD CHANGES

I flew up into a sitting position, drenched in a cold sweat and barely catch my breath. I looked at the clock as I hyperventilated—5:10. The Nemesis had made quick work of me on this night. All night I had trouble getting to and staying asleep. He showed his skeletal face almost constantly from the time I closed my eyes through the night. Something in me had known this would happen. He had been accompanied not only by the other man, but there was another presence. I could not put my finger on it; I had no visual evidence as to what was there, but it was there and it was strong. It had been a few nights since the investigation at Shane's house. From the first night we got home, I had been dealing with these issues constantly. For the life of me, I could not sleep peacefully, and it began to take a toll on my ability to function throughout the day. I felt beat up. I had reviewed most of the data we collected during the investigation and had been blown away by everything we had captured. In a sense, I was shocked and even afraid of what would come next, but at the same time, I did feel like the experiment accomplished what I had hoped. We had close encounters with many different energies while we were in the home that night and judging by the change in my overall mood and inability to sleep well throughout the night, I knew that something had changed.

I knew, whether I wanted to admit it or not, that something had changed with my surroundings since I had conducted the Ganzfeld Experiment. I cannot say that I necessarily regretted it because I felt like it was productive. However, I knew I may have opened a can of worms that I was possibly not prepared to deal with. I have not conducted the experiment during an investigation since that night and would definitely think very hard before ever attempting it again. Sometimes as humans, we do not understand the depth of what we are dealing with. We all go through life believing what we can understand and see in front of us, but we all have difficulty understanding or coming to grips with anything that may not be right in front of our face or obvious. I believe the mind is a very powerful thing and will always look for ways to expand my mind in order to find answers to questions that seem to evade us on many levels.

Snort had told me that since we got home that night, he and his wife Jenn, who was pregnant with my niece at the time, had both been seeing a lot of shadowy movement throughout their house, even mostly through the corner of their eyes. Even my other niece had informed them she had been seeing things in her room. I began to get a little worried, and a big part of me was just waiting for Jason to tell me a similar tale. Sure enough, within a few days, Jason had told me that activity in his home had also picked up. His wife, Sarah, had noticed this as well. They had always known there was a presence in their home, but they typically kept that to themselves. He made it clear that everything in the house felt different. What I did not know is whether or not these changes had happened purely because we were the three that participated in the experiment or not. That was my first thought, considering Jared and Dr. Joseph had reported nothing out of the ordinary.

The dreams I had been having were different. I felt like there was something lurking in the shadows, something overwhelming and large. I did not know if it was a physical presence or if it was just a change in the surrounding energy. The dreams had become nearly unbearable, and constant. I had no idea what to do about it. I prayed, as I always do, for protection and at this point in this case, it was becoming more and more clear that I needed protection. It felt like something was closing in on me. I had no idea what it was, but there was not just a creepy presence—it felt like something was trying to get me. Normally my nightmares would feel as though people I loved were the ones in trouble or there was a general uneasiness with the entire environment within the dream. Now it had changed. I felt like I was in danger.

I got dressed and headed to work after the awakening I had dealt with that night and all of a sudden the Ghost Box sitting in my back seat came on. It was very strange; I was surprised that this was even possible. I quickly looked in the back seat and anticipated something lying on top of the device that could have pressed the power button. That was not the case; it was sitting on the seat and nothing was touching it, but it was on. As soon as I picked the device up to turn it off, a distinct laughing sound came from the box. The channels were not scanning, but this laugh did not sound human and it was repetitive. It only happened when I picked the box up. I quickly turned the device off and tried to ignore what had happened. I went about my normal business.

As soon as I got to work, I sent Jason a message on the computer and let him know we needed to have lunch that day so we could talk. He agreed.

"Something seems to be stalking you, I don't know what it is, but it seems very strong," Jason told me as we ate our lunch. I am always shocked when Jason can feel these things, and my confidence in his abilities grows every day. He was right. I could feel something stalking me, and it wasn't the Nemesis or the other man. It was something else. He could also see in my eyes how drained I was and knew I was not sleeping well.

"No shit, and you don't know what it is? I am always feeling like I am being watched and have no desire to sleep because I know what is waiting for me," I told him in an almost desperate tone.

"Yeah, things have been creepy at my house too," Jason said in a very calm tone.

"So you, me, and Snort all have been experiencing shit since we got home. We are also the three that conducted the experiment. Do you think that is what is going on? Did we invite something in? Do you feel like it's dangerous?" I peppered him with questions, knowing he was the only person I knew who could truly get a handle on these things.

"I don't know what it is, but I am confident it had something to do with the Ganzfeld Experiment for sure. I don't think it was necessarily invited, but it was definitely given free rein when we conducted the experiment. I can't say whether it is dangerous or not as of yet; I do get the feeling it is a physical being though. I do feel like there could be something physical that may happen, I don't know if it is looking to hurt someone or just looking to give some kind of message." Jason tried to give me confidence, and he knew something he was not telling me. My assumption was he had a good idea what he thought it was, but I did not press him at the time because in a way

I simply wanted to stop thinking about it for a while and just finish our lunch.

That evening, I decided to go to Snort's house to talk to him and Jenn about the things that had been going on in their house. They had also seen and heard things off and on since they had moved in about a year prior to this case. They said things felt different.

"No bullshit. Since we got back, it has been obvious. Something has been just darting from one room to another and up and down the hallways. It's freaking weird, dude," Snort told me.

I told him about my dreams, and Snort said he had not been sleeping very well either. Because of his back problems, it was not out of the ordinary that he had trouble sleeping, but he did say this was different. It wasn't the typical comfort issues with his sleep, he was also having some pretty strange dreams. He decided he and Jenn would do a blessing on the house and hoped that would help calm things down. They would typically cleanse their home on a regular basis by burning sage and praying the rosary. Burning sage is said to help relieve a location of spirits and it allows them to move on and puts up something of a force field against darker energy that wants to linger in a home or a building. We had used a similar method in home cleansings on cases in the past, but we had also learned that this was not always an effective method of cleansing. Sometimes it had no ability to get rid of some darker energies that were more persistent about staying where they were.

There are dozens of methods to perform a cleansing on a home. A lot of times we would simply discuss what we believed to be there, which would typically lead us down the path to finding what we hoped would be a good cleansing method. They were always pretty good about doing that sort of thing, and it seemed to help out. We were all hopeful that would be the case this time. I gave them and my niece and nephews a hug and headed home.

Within a few minutes of leaving my brother's house, I got a call from him. I answered expecting Snort to tell me that I had left something behind, but he needed to tell me something else. He explained that a couple minutes after I left, a few very strange things happened.

"Something seemed to fly through the back door and zip through the room, and I saw what looked like something glowing fly quickly through the whole main level. When it zipped through the front door, there was some kind of crackle outside. It almost sounded like lightning! That was it, I haven't heard anything since, but that was absolutely insane dude!" Snort was obviously shaken. Jenn confirmed what he saw and was just thankful that all the kids had been upstairs playing.

They informed me they were going to do the blessing that night, and I could not agree more. Whatever had just happened was crazy. Of course, I wish I had been there to see it, but at the same time, I was just glad nobody was hurt. I was hoping the blessing would help them and help things calm down. I gave them my love and headed home looking forward to another restless night.

The nightmares were kept at bay that night, and I felt like a new man the next day. It is amazing what some rest can do. Snort reported that nothing out of the ordinary had happened since the incident last night. They had done the cleansing and felt pretty good about where things stood now. Jason also told me that things seemed to have calmed down a little in his house. I was starting to feel a little better. For almost a week, it seemed as though some type of energy had been wreaking havoc in our lives. I was hopeful it had passed and we would all be able to move on. It seemed with each investigation at Shane's home, the creepy occurrences and feelings we brought home with us went up a notch. This time, we seemed to be surrounded for almost a week but we had hoped whatever it was had dissipated.

That evening I received a call from Betty, Shane's girlfriend. Betty informed me that they had been over to the house to clean up. We had planned on heading back to Haun's Mill this upcoming weekend and had scheduled another trip to Shane's on the following weekend. Betty was frantic and explained that regardless of what needed to be cleaned or moved, she and Shane had decided never to go back into the house. I did my best to talk to her and try to keep her calm. Betty explained that they had seen something and Shane had actually captured it on video with his cell phone. Of course, I asked Shane to send me the video as quickly as he could. I let them know that steering clear of the house was a good decision. They were thankful for my attention and let me know they would send me the video as soon as they could. I told them we would be back down in a week and a half, and at this point we wanted to do one more thorough investigation, then we would put our heads together and figure out, if possible, what approach to take to rid the house of this dark energy. Of course, throughout the entire process, I have been discussing certain options with Jason, but at this point, we wanted just a little more confirmation to make sure we were positive as to what we were dealing with before we went about trying to rid the home of it. I knew we could make matters much worse if we were wrong, so I erred on the side of caution and thought one more good investigation may give us what we needed.

I opened up the forty-five second video and was absolutely stunned by what I saw. Shane was standing in his kitchen with the lights off, although I could see as he slowly panned from one side of the kitchen to the other, the lights were on in the living room and front entrance area. He pointed the camera to his right and there seemed to be some kind of orb that slowly moved from the entrance to the kitchen and slowly floated toward a china cabinet that stood against the large wall of the kitchen. There were two candles lit, and as they came into frame the orb seemed to slowly float between the two candles and disappeared into the cabinet and then into the wall. Shane then slowly panned toward the entrance of the kitchen that pointed to the living room area and the front entrance that included the main stairway to the top level of the house. As the camera caught the light of the living room and hallway area, there was a very large figure that moved calmly from the living room toward the staircase, and then disappeared. The most frightening thing about this figure was it did not look like a shadow or a person or anything. The only way to describe it was a huge figure that seemed to be cloaked in a large black gown of sorts, and it looked as though there was some type of hood covering the figure. The figure stood taller than the entryway to the living room, and it seemed to simply glide across the hallway and disappeared into the staircase. The angle Shane had shot the video from gave a pretty clear view of this figure, but I could not see exactly what happened to the figure once it left the frame. The video suddenly got choppy and ended. Shane had originally seen the orb but he and his girlfriend never said anything about this figure. They apparently did not see it, but it was very clear.

This monstrosity of a figure struck me like a bolt of lightning between the eyes. I had no idea how to react because my gut immediately told me this was the being we had been looking for all along. It did not look human—it looked more like a stereotypical depiction of the Grim Reaper. I was officially freaked out and knew this was the way this energy would present itself to me.

I showed the video to several people I trusted and nobody could explain what it was. It clearly was something very large, and it definitely moved. I had first tried to dismiss it as the camera moving and somehow catching an object at an odd angle that may have given the illusion of the figure. Everyone who looked at it simply could not make that determination. I knew of course I had to do experiments when we went back down there to make sure, but this was so obvious I simply could not debunk it without feeling like I was inventing a reason to put my head in the sand to ignore something that was right in front of my face. There is a dangerous line between keeping an open mind and denying something that may as well slap you in the face. In this case, I simply could not turn a blind eye. It was way too obvious. I had been to that house enough times to know it like the back of my hand and having the lights on where they were, it seemed that Shane had caught something red-handed as it moved freely through the main level of the house and seemed to disappear into the wall.

At this point, I could not get back to Shane's house fast enough. It seemed like something had declared war on us—and it had been apparent for some time that war had been waged well before we ever arrived. This thing knew who we were and why we were there. It seemed as though the intent was to make sure we were not able to interrupt its reign over the house. It was crystal clear that we were in the middle of a very serious situation, and my only hope was that we were protected, and we would be able to eventually bring peace to Shane and his family. I was determined to do whatever necessary to accomplish this seemingly gargantuan feat.

I was not sure what it was; my alarm had not had a chance to go off, but I sat up in bed wide awake. I decided I would just get ready for the day and get a move on.

I was in the shower and all of a sudden I felt uncomfortable. I remembered being a child, specifically the times I would be down in the basement and as I would come up the stairs I would suddenly get an overwhelming feeling of panic. I would then sprint up the stairs from the basement as though if I hadn't, something would have come after and gotten me. I had that same feeling of panic right now. I didn't know what to do, but as I was washing my hair, I did it quickly. Suddenly, as I was rinsing off, there was a scream. A loud and female scream that sounded as though it was just on the other side of the shower curtain. It was blood-curdling and sounded like someone being scared to death or even tortured. It lasted about three seconds and in my panic I almost fell out of the shower. I quickly opened my eyes and threw open the shower curtain to find nothing. My heart almost beat out of my chest. Was I going crazy? I felt like it. I proceeded to go about my day in what felt like a zombie-like state. I was shocked at what I had heard and all I could think about was the story I had been told about the one and only thing Shane had ever heard in his life. I felt like I just experienced the exact same thing and it had me frightened to the point where I felt like I was truly in danger. I had no idea if I should tell anyone about this for fear that they would think I was quickly losing my mind. As I write this, this is the first I have ever spoken of this incident. Right this very second, my skin is crawling and the goosebumps are enormous up and down my body. This may have been the scariest moment of my entire life. And it was real.

Thirteen

BACK TO HAUN'S MILL

We needed a little break from Shane's house. I know there are different opinions as to how to approach a private home case and how many investigations are required before attempting to rid a home of activity. There are also differing opinions as to how to go about this. Since I established my team, I took it upon myself to decide what we do and when we do it. I contend that before you attempt to rid a home of activity, you need to know what it is. Many would say this is simply impossible. I understand that, but I disagree. I have made a point of surrounding myself with talented people who give me the ability to assess a situation from every angle. I look at it from a logical point of view and listen to the opinions of scientists and mediums, then follow the evidence we uncover during investigations and our data review afterward. In the end, this is not an exact science and as long as people are investigating the paranormal, there will be differing opinions regarding methodology.

I determined we needed a break partly because Shane had left the house in his rearview for at least the time being, if not permanently. I also kept in mind all the crazy shit that had been going on with most of my team since our most recent investigation. We needed a little break before making our final push to get rid of this dark force that had infested Shane's home. So I was excited to get the rest of the team out to Haun's Mill. Of course Jared and I had an interesting, to say the least, scouting trip, but I was confident that this time would be different. I tried to learn a lesson from that debacle that nearly ended my car's valiant life. So we hit the road and looked forward to a relaxing and adventurous day and night.

"So what is the reasoning behind coming to this place? How did you find it? What's the story?" my brother asked as we were heading down the highway and had our fill of fart jokes. He decided to get a little prepared for what we were about to go do.

"Well buddy, I was just doing research on ghost towns because I think we need to focus on finding reasons to be at a location and not base our investigations on reported activity. I did not find any reports of activity, but am going by the actual story to see if we can anticipate whether activity may happen, and this seemed like a great place to start," I explained to everyone as they listened intently.

You see, since the day I decided to begin investigating the paranormal, I had a big picture vision of my goals. Number one, always first and foremost, was to help those in need. The idea that so many people out there were living in fear in their own homes was simply too much to bear. I decided that I would educate myself in any way I could and find a way to help as many people as possible. Secondarily, I wanted to tell stories to people of lost history. This country has been around since the beginning of time, at least the land has, and it is drenched in history. All too often, this history is overlooked due to a short-sighted view of this great land we inhabit. Just because there is a jail sitting on a location, it must be haunted? Just because there is a cemetery on a plot of land, it must be haunted? All haunted locations must be within these narrow confines? Seriously, if you believe this type of thing really exists, isn't it a little naive to think that it only exists in these designated areas? It's unbelievable to me that so many teams out there waste so much time investigating these famously haunted locations when they could be venturing out into the unknown and finding places that could help advance our field of research. This was my second objective, to open people's minds and allow them to think outside the box. Just because I could not just Google and find pages of reported activity at Haun's Mill did not mean there was no activity at the site. We had the people and the equipment, so why the hell wouldn't we go and find out for ourselves?

As we drove down the dusty dirt road in the middle of nowhere in North Central Missouri, I decided I would explore the other road that seemed to approach the memorial site in hopes we could avoid having to dig ourselves out of another mud hole on this day. I took a left instead of driving straight and sure enough, we were led on a pretty decent dirt road right to the memorial site and found a place to park the car.

Jared looked at me and simply said, "Dude, what the hell" as we pulled in, and we all got a good laugh as everyone was well aware of the now notorious story of him being balls deep in mud on our scouting trip. The day was off to a really good start.

We arrived in the middle of the afternoon, so we had more than enough time to explore this vast area in hopes we could come across some type of sign of where all the gruesome events in this area had taken place.

I decided to navigate through a field that had previously been overgrown, but had since been manicured to the point where it was very easy to explore. According to all the historical maps I could find, this field was a big part of Haun's Mill and I was hoping to come across some sign of the mysteriously missing well that all the innocent people had been cast into upon their demise. Jason, Jared, and Snort headed off into the woods along the creek that spread far enough that it was almost a small river. The water level was pretty far down because of the seemingly endless drought we had all summer and it carried over into the fall.

I carried the K-II with me because that device seemed to be very in tune with energy bursts we had come across on our scouting trip so I was hopeful that it would lead me where I needed to be. We had radios, but the fellas were nowhere to be found as they had disappeared into the thick woods. I made several trips around this field in a combing pattern and came across several interesting spots. Three sites actually looked like archaeological digs had taken place, so I was endlessly curious who had conducted these digs and what they may have found. I made a note to do some research on this when I got home.

I had more than enough of this field, which was about the size of a football field, so I decided to contact the guys. They said they were on the other side of the creek. I decided I to join them, but I had no idea where to cross. I began to follow the creek and came across a very large tree that had fallen, forming a bridge to the other side. I figured this must be where they crossed, although I was a little surprised, as it looked pretty dangerous. To be honest, it did not cross my mind that the fellas would risk life and limb to cross a creek.

"Screw it," I thought as I stepped up onto the large tree and began to walk across. The tree stood about fifteen feet above trickling water that was surrounded by rocks and debris from other fallen bushes and trees. I knew if I fell, I was pretty much hosed—a broken leg was the best-case scenario. Nonetheless, I put one foot in front of the other and made my way across the tree to the other side of the creek. I maneuvered my way across and got to the other side and then had to navigate through all the branches that had dug into the ground, which proved to be tricky. Once I got up there I radioed the boys and asked them where I needed to go to find them. They gave me vague directions, but what stood out was this beautiful meadow I found myself standing in the middle of. It was breathtaking; all of a sudden, I felt like I shared Sherwood Forest with Robin Hood. The surrounding hills that stood as steep as I could imagine and this wide open area that was mesmerizing. I just had a sense of peace come over me and made my way toward the guys.

As we all discussed some of the interesting things we had found during our exploration, we knew there was something mystical about the area, although we collected nothing but a few hits on the EMF detectors. We just took the time to take in the sights and feelings of the place. Jason felt a lot of different emotions. We decided to head back to the rally point and I led everyone to the tree that we had to cross.

"Dude, are you crazy???" Jared exclaimed to me as Jason laughed hysterically.

"What?" I asked him.

"You crossed that freaking tree??? You are insane!" All three of them chuckled as they apparently had found a slightly easier method to cross the creek about a quarter mile down the way.

"Well, it wasn't too bad. It's a little slippery at spots," I told them. As they kept walking downstream, I felt the screw-it-all attitude come over me and would prove to them how easy this trek across the tree actually was. I crossed back over and my brother followed suit. Jared and Jason made it quite clear how jacked in the head they thought we were and headed upstream to make their way back to us. My brother and I slowly made our way across the huge log and had a good chuckle over the next twenty minutes we waited for Jared and Jason.

"Wusses," my brother and I agreed halfheartedly. He and I made our way back to the field as we waited for the guys and I took him to the dig site.

"That is awesome," Snort told me as he jumped right into the three-foot hole that had previously been completely hidden by the overgrowth. He could not resist the urge to start digging around although his efforts were fruitless as he found nothing. It wasn't long until Jason and Jared caught up with us.

We went back down toward the creek area after a little more exploring and Jason and I had split up from Snort and Jared. They were exploring the memorial area while Jason and I headed back toward the tree that sprawled across the creek.

"I feel something out of the ordinary here. In this area, I don't know what it is, but it feels like panic," Jason said, as I took a step up onto the tree.

I then took a few steps out onto the tree and suddenly am overcome with the feeling that I am deathly afraid to be standing there. The two previous times as I had crossed the tree, I had no fear whatsoever; now I suddenly felt like I was afraid of heights and was all but frozen.

I hear Jason clicking away with his badass camera as he wanted to take some pictures of me "in action."

"Dude, I suddenly feel like I am frozen, like I am scared to death of falling," I told Jason and as I was saying this, the K-II in my hand went absolutely crazy. I had seen a few small fluctuations here and there throughout the day, but all of a sudden, the lights came on as strong as they could.

"Keep taking pictures around me, dude. Something is wrong," I said as he clicked away with his DSLR camera.

After a couple more minutes, I came back down and rejoined Jason, and we discussed the difference in the over-all feeling I had between now and the previous trips across the tree. He pointed out that he felt like we were being watched by something nearby. He pointed to the area down near the creek and we both started taking pictures in that direction. Upon review of the pictures later on, we did notice that as opposed to previous pictures taken in the exact same location, there were visible orbs in a couple of the pictures that we had taken right where Jason said he felt we were being watched from. I do not put much stock in orbs that show up in pictures; I simply make note of when they show up during an uptick in activity or when we are investigating odd feelings that we have.

"This place is awesome!" my brother exclaimed as we all joined back up in anticipation of the sun going down in a few minutes.

All of us had a pretty deep-seated desire to explore and this place was perfect because it provided not only the ability to climb and hike, but it also had provided us with evidence that something out of the ordinary was going on. As the sun dropped beneath the distant hills, darkness blanketed the area in no time. The overall feeling of the entire area changed almost immediately when the sun went down. Such an open and serene place now had an overall feeling of dread that seemed to come hand in hand with the darkness that covered the land. All of a sudden, a place of such peace simply felt like it was a place that was in total chaos.

After a couple hours of exploring the area after the sun had gone down, I was using the RT-EVP device, which at the time was brand new and had not been around long enough for any evidence it produced to be deemed reliable. This device, I should explain, has a built-in microphone that records audio that we cannot hear with our own ears. The microphone is very sensitive and has a slight delay in it playing back the surrounding audio through the earbuds I was wearing. So I am hearing absolutely everything going on, but on a couple-second delay.

A few very interesting things came across as I listened, I felt like I had picked up a name as I was asking who was following us: *"Josiah."* Jason looked at me like he had seen a ghost as I repeat what I had just heard.

"I picked that name up several times earlier, remember?" Jason asked as I clearly remembered talking to him about several names that had been historically linked to the location. The thing is, I kept these names quiet in Jason's presence because I wanted to see if he picked up on any of the names or energy that could be linked to the Haun's Mill tragedy. I had told him nothing about the location, and one of the first things he picked up on earlier in the day was the name Josiah.

We made our way back to the trail that went from the memorial stone to the creek and decided we would conduct a Ghost Box session there.

"Who is here?" my brother asked and got an unexpected and immediate reply that seemed to come through the scanning channels of white noise: *"Go away!! Fuckers!"* The words rang loud and clear as we all jumped a little.

"Shhh." I told everyone to get quiet as I thought I heard something, and sure enough, we all began to hear what sounded like someone running along the creek bed in the very shallow water. We then heard what sounded like footsteps in the leaves surrounding the area on both sides of the creek. One set of footsteps that were very obvious came from the side of the creek we were on, so I gave them all what may have looked like a military hand gesture and we slowly headed in that direction without saying anything. We came up through the path that led to the creek and headed toward what sounded like several people bolting back and forth through the leaves just about fifty yards away. We made our way over there and suddenly Snort grabbed my arm to stop me, and he immediately pointed to our left.

"Buddy," he whispers, "I swear I just saw two shadows bolt from behind one tree across to another, right over there; watch."

We all paused and suddenly heard the all-too familiar sound of a pack of coyotes screaming through the silent night air. We all puckered a little bit and looked at one another. Almost immediately, I saw what looked like a shadow in the exact area Snort had pointed at. I slowly made my way into the wooded area and the guys slowly spread out so we could cover a little more ground. We were all armed with cameras and/or recorders in hopes of capturing something that was lurking in the darkness.

After a few more minutes of searching for this shadowy figure, things seemed to calm down a little. We could no longer hear the footsteps that had previously surrounded us. We all took the opportunity to catch our breath and have a good old-fashioned "Holy shit that just happened" discussion near the car. Of course the painful screaming of the coyotes, now a little closer, had become a focal point of our ongoing conversation. Looking back, we had an absolutely incredible time at Haun's Mill on this evening. It turned out to present some very compelling things and in the end, it was exactly what we were looking for—an open area to explore and bond together. Snort is and always will be my brother, but on this night, it was reiterated that the four of us were bonded as closely as we could be and there was nothing that could break these bonds.

As we packed up the car and headed out, we were having a good laugh about all the events and were discussing the fact that what we do goes so much deeper than to simply put "evidence" on a website or play the popularity game on all the social media sites. Yes, eventually some of these things may come into play, but for now, I simply wanted to get our methods of research down to a science, and this place lent credibility to my theories. I think everyone understood now.

As Jason quickly flipped through the pictures he had taken after he had uploaded them to his laptop, we saw the most outrageous thing we had ever captured with a camera. As I had been standing on the tree over the creek earlier in the day, I felt the overwhelming feeling of discomfort and thoughts that I should not be standing there because I was in danger. What showed up clear as day in this picture had us all at a loss for words. I was simply standing on the log and had my focus on what was in front of me, and there was a perfectly visible face that lay over mine in the picture. We were quickly able to rule out a double exposure because of the type of camera Jason had been using. The thing was, double exposure or not, this face was perfectly visible and very different from mine. The face had an elongated nose and pointy chin. For a moment, I wondered if it could have been my Nemesis. We could clearly see the dark eyes, and it looked as though this rough-looking man was wearing a hat that seemed to perfectly fit the period during which the massacre had taken place at Haun's Mill. There was no body, simply a detailed face that overlay my own, and as we zoomed in on the picture, it was obvious the face had not only lay over mine, but it made mine disappear. You could not see any details of my face because they were blocked by the details of the man who kept me company on this fallen tree that stood about fifteen feet above the creek. I was mesmerized by it; I simply could not stop trying to understand what we had captured in this picture. Was this "Josiah"? Was this the source of the threatening voice that had come clearly through the Ghost Box earlier in the evening? Why did his presence make me so uncomfortable on the tree? Did he have bad intentions for me, or was he trying to warn me and let me know that I was in a dangerous situation? I had no idea what to make of it, but I could not stop looking at it.

"What the hell is that?!" I nearly screamed at Jason as I saw something that leapt off the screen at me.

"That is a freaking face on my face, dude! That is right when I felt that creepy feeling while I was standing on the log!"

"Oh my God, dude, that is unreal!" he muttered as Jared and Snort went to see what the fuss is about.

"Holy shit! Haha!" Snort exclaimed as he almost wrecked the car.

"Dude, no way," Jared threw in his thoughts on the matter.

We continued onward toward home and were all dumbfounded by everything that had happened. We had seen and heard unexplainable things all night and suddenly we were face to face, literally, with the face of a man that clearly was not in our physical presence when the picture was taken. At least we could not see him with our own eyes, but it had become very clear to me that he was there, and my body and mind knew it. This picture changed something in me. It taught me an extremely valuable lesson about paying attention to my body and mind. It is all too easy to dismiss a feeling when you are exploring a "creepy" place, but without jumping to conclusions, an investigator should always pay attention to the internal feelings he or she is experiencing. Our minds and bodies are extremely important and powerful tools during these investigations. It is very easy to forget this fact, and this picture gave me confidence in knowing that my feelings were spot on. I had been on that tree several times and felt perfectly comfortable, and the one time I was on it and felt like I should not have been, this comes up and slaps me in the face. I was simply enamored with the picture and to this day hold this picture close to my heart as a turning point in my life as an investigator. There will always be someone who wants to find a reason to debunk the picture, but being that I was there and experienced the entire thing, there is no way anyone could convince me that I was not in the presence of this man. What his intentions were, I cannot say. But I thank him, whoever he is, for opening my eyes in a whole new way.

BBQ

The next day we had all calmed down a little and went about our normal Sunday following an investigation. My brother and I were to go over to my parent's house that day for a BBQ. It was a beautiful, early fall day and we were surrounded by family and the kids running around acting crazy as they are so talented at doing. I had come in from the back yard where everyone was socializing, and I noticed my dad standing and looking intently out the front door through the screen.

"You okay, Pa (as the three of us boys lovingly call him)?" I asked as it was apparent he was in deep concentration on something.

He turned and looked at me with a pale look on his face, "I just saw a head or a face that was hiding behind your car across the street," he said with very little emotion.

This is where I need to point out that my father is the last man on Earth that would ever claim to see anything such as a ghost. He grew up in a devoutly Catholic home and they did not spend time talking about or deciding whether or not they believed in such things. My dad is a very realistic and levelheaded man. Simply put, he is one of the most incredible people I have ever known. His integrity could never be questioned by anyone. The fact that he said what he saw to me told me that I immediately needed to pay attention to him—and his word was set in stone. If he said he saw a face hiding behind my car, that is exactly what he saw.

He went on to explain that he'd been watching it for a couple minutes. It was not a situation where he saw something quickly out of the corner of his eye—he had stood there staring at something for a couple minutes until I came in and broke his concentration. He described almost exactly what we had seen on the previous night following our investigation in the picture. The face of a man with distinct features who looked like he wore an old period hat, a farmer's hat, from the 1800s. I was astonished and I immediately bolted out to my car with my camera. Snort joined me shortly after I got out there and began taking pictures. None of the pictures I took had anything out of the ordinary in them. Snort and I discussed the fact that he and his wife Jenn had also felt some strange things going on in and around their house after he got home the night before.

We went on about our day and enjoyed our time spent together as a family and the great company. However, I believe this very morbid occurrence was always in the back of all our minds for the remainder of the day. My parents have always accepted what I do as an investigator, they have always supported me, and they understood that I simply have to do what I have to do.

I would go back to my parents' house a few days later and my mom took me to their back yard because she wanted to show me what my dad had gone out and purchased. In the far corner of the yard stood a gargoyle. This symbol that has stood for centuries, thought to ward off evil, was now a staple in my parents' back yard. Gargoyles are demonic-looking stone carvings of creatures that are typically used by the Catholic Church to give a visual reminder for those who conduct themselves in an evil manner of what may await them in the afterlife. This is one interpretation of their usefulness anyway. These stone creatures have been used by many different religions for many different reasons over many centuries, but putting two and two together from what had happened over the weekend, it was quite obvious what my dad intended this creature to do. It was there to insure he and my mother, and their property and home were not bothered by any potential spirits that may be tagging along with their adventurous son, whom they love so much.

In all honesty, I could not blame him for a second. As a matter of a fact, I was happy about it. The last thing I have ever wanted was to put any of my family members or friends in the way of whatever energy that may be following me around. It had become very apparent over the past several weeks that it was not uncommon, and at this point expected that I was very prone to being followed by something, or someone.

I had to set all this aside for the time being and bring my focus back to the main task at hand. We would be heading to Shane's in five short days and I had a lot of preparation work to finish up. There was one thought that seemed to keep ringing in my head though: "What have I gotten myself into? Better yet, what had I gotten all of us into?"

Fourteen

THE RECKONING

It was a beautiful fall Saturday afternoon when I showed up at Jared's house to pick him up. We geared up and set out to Shane's house. Jason and Snort could not make the trip that weekend. Jason had some family business to tend to, and Snort could not leave Jenn as she was due to give birth to my second niece at any time. He did not feel like being several hours away was a good choice. Right now, with everything going on since our last trip to Shane's house, I actually thought it was a good thing that Jason and Snort were not going to be directly involved because of the escalation in our personal lives since the last investigation. This also gave me an opportunity to work with a friend of mine and his team that I had gotten to know from a distance for several months.

Russell Keeler and his wife, Julie, and adult daughter, Courtney (not to be confused with my brother, Snort), would be driving up from Arkansas to join us. I had never worked with Russ and his crew before, but I was confident I'd be happy to work with him. I am always on the lookout for new friends and great investigators to work with. I am very careful about the people I surround myself with, but I had a very good feeling about not just the type of investigator Russ seemed to be, but the type of person. He is a very down to earth and lighthearted person and I was really excited to meet him and his family. I knew bringing them into the investigation at Shane's was a good idea because it would bring a female perspective that had been missing in our previous investigations in the house with the exception of Claire from Jeremiah's team, but it had been a while, so I was curious what would happen. Also, I have a more in-your-face investigation style and knew that Russ took a little more laid-back approach. I knew he would bring something really good to the equation.

As Jared and I set out on the road, we got to talking about everything that had been going on recently. I told him about what had happened at my parents' house and all the odd activity that had been going on at several different locations involving Jason and Snort. To put his mind at ease, I reconfirmed that they were not missing tonight's investigation because of all the side effects; he knew I wouldn't knowingly put him in an uncomfortable situation. After I finished explaining everything to him, Jared decided to share some interesting information with me. He explained that he and his wife had been arguing a lot more than normal. They were usually very non-combative people, but recently they were both on edge seemingly all the time. The thought had crossed his mind that because she was so standoffish about him making all these trips and being involved with the investigations had her to the point of taking issue with the entire thing. I could completely understand what he was saying and reiterated that I had told everyone involved from the very beginning that family and priorities would always come first. I would always respect everyone's situation and would never question their motives or their dedication. I never want to see any of my brothers having trouble at home. It did not help matters that Jared's wife was also due to have their third child any day at that point. We always found it very cool that both Jared and Snort would be welcoming in a new addition to the family within a few days of each other. I knew Jared's wife was not a fan of him coming that night, but in true Jared fashion, he set everything aside and came with me, knowing I was on my own if he did not come along.

As Jared and I arrived, Russ and his family had just pulled up, so it was great timing. Russ was the founder of a group based out of Siloam Springs, Arkansas, called After Midnight Paranormal Investigations. As I said before, I had not had a chance to work with him before, but upon meeting them, I knew I was right to invite them to Shane's house. Russ is a very big guy and his wife and daughter as sweet and lovely as can be. I introduced myself and Jared, and we all were looking forward to the night's investigation. We all hit it off famously and Russ and his family had a great attitude and an infectious energy that I knew would bode well for the evening.

I received a text from Shane shortly after I let him know we had arrived, and he wanted to stop by to again show me exactly where he was when he had recorded the video showing the huge figure. I was taking Russ and company through the house to tell them the reports and experiences we had already collected from our previous investigations. I had explained that the encounters that had died down recently with a woman whom we thought to be named Emily were upstairs and near the staircase. I took my time walking them through the house, but avoided taking them to the basement right away.

Shane arrived and was excited to see Jared and me, and he introduced himself to Russ and his family. Shane immediately took me to the kitchen to show me exactly what happened when he recorded the video earlier in the week. Shane seemed very jittery just being in the house, so we decided to go ahead and do what we needed to do quickly, as he had made it very clear that he did not want to be there too long. My one suspicion as to the validity of Shane's video was whether or not he happened to be standing in such a spot that he may have somehow recorded something that was sticking out from the wall. I thought it was unlikely but certainly possible. The house, particularly the kitchen, is overloaded with trinkets and items hanging on the walls, and a lot of them were odd so they could project an odd shape when using cameras in the darkness. Sure enough, where Shane had been standing, I was able to immediately confirm there was no way anything was in the way or had been recorded to create some type of matrix effect. This is a common effect that can make people believe they are seeing something that is not actually there for a number of reasons. For example, a picture like the one Jason took of me at Haun's Mill could be said by anyone wishing to debunk the authenticity of what showed up as the matrix effect because there was a lot of foliage and debris in the background. The thing was, the details of the face stood out as obvious and were on the front side of my face, so everything in the background could easily be ruled out. Another example would be in Shane's house, if the lights were off in one room and on in another, using a camera could create something solid and with shape that was hanging off or jutting out from the wall where the object hung. This could create any number of shapes. Along with the camera slowly panning from one side of the room to the other, which could make the foreign object appear to be moving, the video could plausibly be debunked.

I set up three different cameras and adjusted my angle and speed of movement of each several times. We also conducted the experiment several times with lights on and off in both rooms, and of course with the lights on in the living room and the lights off in the kitchen. I even asked Shane if I could use his phone to see if I could re-create it with the exact same camera. He happily obliged, but I was unable to come remotely close to re-creating the video. I was completely convinced at that point that we saw what we believed we saw—a huge figure moving from one side of the hallway to the other and seemingly disappearing into the main staircase by the home's front entrance. For the life of me I still had a very difficult time accepting this as complete truth because it was something that I never thought even remotely possible. You have to remember, many times upon seeing or experiencing something new, investigators, if they doing their job properly, will approach every situation not only with an open mind, but a logical one as well. The most exciting thing about being an investigator is coming across something that is simply not logical, or normal. Sometimes it is easy to look past certain things because our minds are trained from a very young age to assume certain things are not possible or not real. That is the beauty of using so much equipment—it allows us to go back and review something recorded so we can confirm or debunk things that we cannot wrap our brains around as it happens. Sometimes you come up unlucky and do not have a good angle on the occurrence; sometimes you are spot on and then you are able to see something that you never thought possible. That was the case with this video. It was a game changer for me; it depicted something I had never seen and never thought possible. It was amazing.

At this point, I went ahead and took Russ and his family to the basement as Jared went out front with Shane, one of his cousins, and Betty to talk before they left for the evening. As I led the way downstairs, Russ is quickly shaken, "What the— sheesh! What the hell was that?" he interjected as I paused about halfway down the stairs and looked up.

"What happened?" I asked.

"I swear I just felt like something grabbed my ankle! Holy shit!" he said with his endearing Southern accent. His demeanor went from happy-go-lucky and upbeat to almost concerned, after just twenty minutes in the house.

I had made a point to make sure they understood that this place was no joke. The thing is, until you experience something in a new location, you are forced to take every report you hear with a grain of salt. That is the only way to keep a level head and objective outlook. Russ was obviously good at what we do, and he was very clear that he felt something grab him.

Suddenly, as we paused to allow Russ to describe what had just happened, our old pal Toby came hauling ass down the stairs and cut right in front of me on the stair beneath my feet. He made his presence and the fact that he had something to tell us very well-known and he would not go unheard on this particular evening. With each slow step I took, Toby seemed to get more aggressive with his need for me to listen and respond to him. By the time I got to the bottom of the stairs he had turned his attention away from me and toward Russ and the girls, as if to say, "Fine, you don't want to listen to me, maybe these people are more intelligent; screw you then." So Toby turned his attention toward them and he was so aggressive with his vocalizations and rebellious stance at the base of the stairs that he almost tripped Russ and the girls up as they slowly made their way down to the bottom and tried to avoid him.

"What a cute kitty!" Julie said in the sweetest way. I found humor in the fact that she said this while Toby was acting like nothing short of the feline version of Cujo.

Both she and Courtney were determined to calm Toby down, so Julie picked him up and before she could even embrace him, he scratched the shit out of her arm. She quickly decided that maybe picking him up was not the best idea. The thing was, I had explained how he acts when people go to the basement. Then again, you have to keep in mind, this is all taking place just minutes after both Julie and Courtney had a lovefest with Toby upstairs just after we had arrived. Simply put, Toby did not want anyone in the basement, and on this night he would not go without being heard.

"Dude, is Shane still here?" I radioed up to Jared.

"Yeah, they are getting ready to take off, why?" he called back down to me.

"I need him to come downstairs and get Toby, he is attacking any of us that try to touch him," I tell Jared and can only imagine the hysterics he must be in after hearing what just came out of my mouth. Within a minute, Jared, Shane, and his girlfriend Betty all made their way to the basement to retrieve a still riled-up Toby.

As Shane picked him up, Toby swiped with fury at him as well and he dropped him to the ground immediately. Shane has a totally panicked look on his face as this was the first time since he had owned Toby that he had ever shown even the slightest bit of aggression toward him. Shane's arm began to bleed where Toby's razor-sharp claws had just made their mark. He then bent down and picked Toby up and quickly rushed upstairs with him much to Toby's chagrin. The entire way upstairs Toby remained violent with his actions and seemingly vulgar with his vocalizations.

"That was exciting; shit," I said to try to lighten the seemingly tense air, and we all got a bit of a chuckle before I finished giving them the tour of the basement.

I took them into the dungeon and they were immediately enthralled by the markings all over the walls. It was something you simply could not look past. The scratches all over the walls seemed to be carved in, and the markings all just gave the room an instantly negative feeling. The fact that this room seemed to serve absolutely no purpose was always one of its more disturbing attributes. So I completed the tour and we headed back upstairs to say our farewell to Shane and his friends and family and make sure we have all the cameras set up so we are ready to begin the investigation.

The mood was actually kept pretty light leading up to the investigation, as it was apparent that the AMPI crew had no problem enjoying what we all did, and they always did their best to have a good time. We all had one final chuckle about the now locked-up monster that was Toby. All the equipment was set up as Jared always showed up and kicked ass when it came to setting up and taking down the equipment. He may have a strange way of detecting threatening energy as his bowels had proven more than once, but he is damn good at what he does. I was very happy about the group we had tonight and felt like it would be a very productive evening.

"I just want to let you guys know that we have been on this case for months and for many reasons, not the least of which is at Shane's request, that I will be turning up the heat tonight. I do not typically provoke in someone's home, but Shane has left this place behind and we need to confront whatever is here, so I will be getting pretty aggressive tonight. I just want you guys to know this is not standard operating procedure," I said, trying my best to explain everything before we got started. I normally deemed it very dangerous and unprofessional to conduct yourself this way in someone's home, but I felt like we had no choice at this point, and time felt like it was running short, so I had to pull out all the stops. I had warned them that the last time we got really aggressive, when Jeremiah and his crew were with us, things started happening almost immediately.

"No worries bro, let's get this started," Russ reassured me that we were all set and ready to get this started.

I began the night with Russ in the basement while the girls and Jared stayed upstairs to try to contact Emily. Russ and I went straight to the dungeon and got to work.

"I brought a new friend with me tonight, do you know him? His name is Russell," I said.

"Oh damn! He's big!" [EVP] An immediate and obviously intelligent response was picked up on my recorder. I would not hear this until I reviewed the audio following the investigation, but I was blown away at how clear this familiar voice was. This fairly deep and almost mocking voice came through loud and clear.

"Why don't you go ahead and show me what you can do?" Russ asked, as we both tried to get a feel for the room on this night.

Our inquisition continued for the next half hour, and we felt occasional cold blasts, as I had felt many times before. Russ was perplexed as we had been because there was absolutely not air movement in this dungeon. It was a warm evening, very comfortable; it had no effect on the temperature in the house.

"Come on, I'm here to communicate with you, you're not gonna upset me," Russ said in a calm voice as he was interrupted in mid-sentence by a low guttural growl as we both paused when he finished his sentence.

"Tell me you heard that," I said.

"How could I not? It sounded like it was right next to you," Russ said, confirming exactly what I heard.

I knew there was no way my recorder didn't pick that sound up, so I was excited and it seemed to bring back to light that the feelings we kept getting about something being there with us seemed to be substantiated. Russ and I kept after it for a little while longer just to get an overall feel of the evening and tried to determine whether we may expect the night to be eventful. We had a couple odd fluctuations with the EMF equipment as well and coupling that with the obvious growl we had heard we figured it could be an interesting night.

I kept it in the back of my mind, but carrying over from my dreams the growling sound that I seemingly could not escape seemed to have made itself audible almost immediately once the investigation had began. My gut told me that I would soon find out what had been chasing me in my dreams and why. I honestly knew why, simply put—I had pissed it off and it was not going to allow me to feel like I had any type of strength in the situation. It had let me know early in the evening that it was not to be trifled with. The problem was, I was there to trifle, so trifle I would.

I received a text from Shane that indicated he wanted to come back for a while later in the night with Betty. In a way, I was happy to hear this because the activity had picked up substantially when he joined us in the past. However, I was a little standoffish about it because the last thing I wanted was for him to be negatively affected by whatever I had stirred up. I confirmed a time with him and let everyone know that we had a few hours before they would be joining us. Russ was stoked that they would be joining us, so we decided to keep at it and see what happened between now and then.

Jared and I had gone upstairs for a little bit to see if anything out of the ordinary was going on, since we had not spent much time up there in a while. Everything seemed to be focused on the lower levels of the house, so that is where we spent most of our time. Again on this evening, it seemed that all was quiet on the top level.

"Brandon, you may want to come down here real quick," Russ called to me over the radio, and I let him know we were on our way.

"There are a lot of orbs flying around!" Courtney said in a playful manner, as she and Julie had both seen glowing balls of light floating throughout the main level of the house on several different occasions.

"An orb about the size of my head just flew into the kitchen and right into that wall right there," Julie said as she pointed toward the exact wall that had appeared in Shane's video that included the large figure.

"I saw a couple of them flying through the kitchen area just a minute ago, and I was just looking down there through the hallway," Russ told me, confirming they were seeing oddly shaped orbs throughout the house and they were not only visible on the cameras, but with their own eyes. It is not too often that you see a random ball of energy floating around with your own eyes, let alone several of them in a short period of time.

"I guarantee you will be able to see that on camera," she reiterated as Jared and I made our way to the DVR system. The girls continued their EVP session in the kitchen in hopes of capturing something on audio that would let us know what was going on. Russ went upstairs for a while to check out the upper level, and right as he reached the top of the stairs he hollered down to us.

"I just saw something like a shadow figure go across the steps as I looked down from the top," he said calmly.

It seemed like there were many outwardly audible sounds on this evening as well as an abundance of visuals that were beginning to let me know that whatever was here was absolutely not going to be shy tonight. I was excited. I had Jared rewind the DVR several minutes until we reached the spot on the video that they had described. Sure enough, we could very clearly see down the main entrance hallways that led to the kitchen and as Courtney stood in the kitchen, a very large and bright light floated into the kitchen and immediately into the wall they had pointed out. When compared to Courtney, it truly was about the size of her head and Jared and I looked at each other with the "oh shit" look and then showed everyone else that the claim had been substantiated. Everyone was amazed at how brazen the energy in the house seemed to be. There was no playing hide-and-seek in this house. If it wanted to be seen, it would be seen. If it wanted to be heard, it would be, and so on.

As the five of us gathered in the living room, we almost immediately began getting spikes on the K-II meter, so we began attempting to communicate. I went about the communication as though we were interacting with Emily, as we thought we had several times before in this general vicinity. All of a sudden Russ looked over his shoulder into the area behind him near the stairs and said, "I just heard that growling sound again; same one we heard earlier."

Sure enough, when I went back and listened to the audio, there was a very distinct growl that came right from the direction Russ had indicated. What we did not hear was the almost immediate EVP that accompanied the growl. In a demanding voice: *"Where's Shane?!"* [EVP]

As we continued our attempt to communicate in the living room, I picked up several more EVPs that I would find upon review. One of them stood out as it seemed to be a cry of desperation in a feminine voice, *"Goooo!!"* [EVP] Once again, it seemed as if Emily was worried about our well-being and was trying everything she could to make us leave. The other sounds captured on the recorders were interesting—some of them sounded like mumbled voices as though there were several right in our presence and they seemed to be having a conversation but the vast majority of the words could not be made out. They were just there. I could not tell if there was anything intelligent being said or not.

After that bit of excitement, I decided to place everyone in their own room so they could all have some quiet time in hopes that something else significant may happen. I made my way to the basement and closed the door behind me so I would go face to face with whatever was down there in pitch blackness. I needed this to happen because I figured there was no other way than to confront whatever had apparently been stalking me, so I headed downstairs alone—determined to figure out if this thing wanted anything specific from me.

Immediately as I arrive in the basement I hear a grumbling sound from the corner that was cluttered with a lot of debris. I could not go back there, but this sounded like something large, so I knew it was not hiding. I could easily hear it, and it was unnerving. I slowly made my way to the location behind the cement wall in the back of the basement where we had previously had a lot of interaction with our equipment. So I adjusted the camera that was sitting on a ledge at the bottom of the stairs so it was pointed in my direction so I could document any response I may receive with the equipment. When I got behind the wall, I set up the K-II as well as a Mel-Meter and an EMF detector. All of these devices detected fluctuations in electromagnetic energy. One would illuminate lights to show the strength of the energy being detected, one alarmed with a beeping sound, and one would show the temperature as well as a digital read-out of what the EMF levels are. Their levels of sensitivity seemed to vary. It seemed as though if one would go off, that did not necessarily mean the others would as well. I had also set up a recorder on the opposite side of the basement as well as two others right next to the meters. I had the Ghost Box with me, but my hope was that I could go without using it. I also set up two mini Maglites so whatever may be down here with me could use those as tools to interact with me.

I got settled behind the wall in the dark and spooky basement. Surrounded by stale air and cobwebs, I could hear shuffling from across the basement. I could not see what was there, but I could feel in my gut that something was lurking in the shadows.

"Well, here I am. How are we gonna do this? I need you to come out and interact with me. Have you been following me?" I began the communication attempt calmly.

"You're fucked." [EVP] I would later find out I picked up on a recorder that sat right in front of me.

"Come make something happen with the equipment; you know how to use it. I am not naive enough to think you are not intelligent. I need to know what your motives are. What do you want to gain from interacting with us? With Shane?" I continued the attempt at communication. Immediately after I got quiet, and I could hear the shuffling again as one of the flashlights began blinking on and off repeatedly. After about five seconds, it turned back to the original off state.

"Alright, well, if you would like to confront me or communicate with me, can you make the K-II lights come on? Can you turn on three lights if you wish to answer yes and two lights for no?" I asked in hopes there would be some semblance of cooperation. At this point, my palms were sweaty and my natural instinct took over, and I was very uncomfortable. I had no idea what to expect and I was seemingly surrounded by a thickness that felt very heavy. I was suddenly having a difficult time breathing and got the feeling in my head that my ears need to pop. I felt like I was on a plane and just hit altitude, and my ears would not pop.

"Death." [EVP] An eerie response I got during review.

"Turn the lights on, jackass!" I raised my voice in a commanding tone in hopes I could convince this being to do something obvious. I was a little rattled, as all five pieces of equipment in front of me turned on or responded in the only way they could. Both flashlights turned on brightly, the EMF detectors were alarming, lighting up and showing digital fluctuations that went from a flat 0.0 to 3.5 all at the same time. Upon review, almost exactly at this time when all the equipment went crazy, I could hear the all-too familiar laughing as though I was being mocked.

"Well, that is something. Can you cooperate with me and impact each piece of equipment when I ask you to?" I asked in my most confident voice. All the equipment went flat as it had been a few short seconds before.

"Does that mean you will cooperate?" I asked once again. No response.

I sat quietly for a second because I heard what sounded like stomping around just above me.

"Are you guys moving around upstairs? Is someone walking in the kitchen?" I radioed up to the crew. I was given an overall response that everyone was still sitting still in their designated locations.

"Are you making that noise?" I asked as one of the flashlights turned on. It stayed on for a few seconds and then went dark once again.

I stood quietly wondering what may be next. All of a sudden, it felt lighter and completely still in my immediate area. I was beginning to wonder if I had experienced everything it was willing to allow me. I tried to remain patient and calm. I stood still, waiting. Waiting.

After about five minutes, I still felt like things have quieted in the basement when all of a sudden, I felt as though a spider spun an enormous web that covered my entire head all at once. I felt like a cobweb net had been dropped on my head and covered me all the way to my neck. I panicked and immediately went to my face to clear off the webs. I was quickly disgusted at the thought of being surrounded by these creatures in the darkness of this disgusting basement. I found nothing anywhere on my face or head. The feeling dissipated almost as quickly as it had come over me. The cobwebs were gone, but my heart was almost beating out of my chest.

"What was that??? Are you serious??? What is your point in doing that?" I asked in a more frantic tone than before. Just as I finished my question, one of the flashlights turned on once again.

"Alright, talk to me!" I requested and was immediately placated by what sounds like a very obvious growl from about five feet in front of me. As I reviewed the recorder, it actually sounded like "NO" or "GO." I could not tell.

This had been one of the most stressful half hours of my life, and one of the most intimidating and eventful I had ever experienced on my own. I was still quite shaken. When I got upstairs, I greeted Shane and his girlfriend, then excused myself to go outside for some air.

It wasn't long after I got outside before I was joined by Jared. It had been a strange night. At that point in the night, everyone seemed a little drained, as was typical after spending an extensive amount of time in this house. It was making perfect sense why Shane had reported feeling depressed and completely drained all the time. It has been my experience that some places do that to people. This house was no different at all.

"You alright, dude?" Jared asked.

"Yeah, just wiped out. This place is a hellhole. How is the wife doing?" I tried to change the subject, as his wife was ready to have their baby any time.

"She's fine. All is well. Stressed though," he told me.

"I understand buddy. We won't be too much longer. We'll hit the road after Shane gets here and spends a little time with us if that's cool."

We continued to shoot the shit for a little while longer as we waited. After about twenty minutes, Shane and his girlfriend showed up and we greeted them. Tommy was perched in his usual lookout spot and was excited to see Shane, who seems to be in good spirits. After Russ and his family came out to join us, we discussed everything before going back into the house. Shane told me that he had felt great ever since he had left the house several days ago. Comparing what he said with how the house made me and seemingly everyone else feel, I was not surprised. We chatted for a few more minutes and then headed into the house to finish off the investigation.

Courtney, Jared, and I headed to the basement while Russ and Julie stayed upstairs with Shane and his girlfriend. We headed down the creaky old stairs and worked our way into the dungeon.

As we got into the dungeon, we set everything up as we were also going to run a Ghost Box session and see if we could get any interaction in real time through the static. We decided we were in a playful mood, so we planned on pushing the envelope a little bit to see what kind of luck we have. It did not take long to get results—pretty freaky results that seemed to prove that something was pissed off.

"Hey! Fuck you!" came from the Ghost Box very clearly. There is what sounds like a male voice that seems to have some vulgar things to say to us as we conduct our communication session.

"Come face to face if you are going to run your mouth, big boy!" I responded as all three of us had picked up clearly what had come from the box. I wanted to give whatever this was a chance to confront us all and give us something definitive that could tell us one way or the other what it was capable of.

"*GET OUT!!!*" the voice in the box screamed.

"You want us out?" I asked in reply.

"*Yes!*" the same clear voice responded.

At this point, we were all pretty excited about the responses. They were timed with our questions or comments and seemed to be intelligently responsive. We were still waiting for something to happen that we could see with our own eyes or feel ourselves, but we also acknowledged that this voice was amazing—it was the exact same voice responding quickly to our comments and questions repeatedly. As the box scanned through all the stations as quickly as it does, what we heard was impossible to mistake for anything other than exactly what it sounded like. And this voice sounded angry.

"I want you to talk to us!" I got more forceful, trying to convince this voice to continue its communication.

"*I did,*" the same voice replied again. At this point, all three of us were impressed—and nearly speechless.

"*Fuck you! Hate!*" the voice continued. The craziest thing about what is going on is that this same exact voice seemed to be getting more and more irritated.

"If you've got a message, go ahead and send it," I commanded the ominous voice.

"Hate," was the simple and immediate reply to my request.

I felt like I was also hearing other voices trying to come through the box, but the one we heard repeatedly was seemingly unable to be interrupted and was very clear.

"How many of you are down here with us?" I asked.

"Three," a different voice came through after a few seconds.

"There are three of you? Can you confirm that by turning on three lights on the meter in my hand?" I tried to incorporate another piece of equipment into the activity we were getting. We were getting a flurry, which was not uncommon, and I knew it would not last too long. Suddenly three lights came on strong on the K-II meter in my hand. I took this as confirmation that the number I had heard come through the box was correct.

A couple minutes passed without any voices coming through the box as we continued to try to communicate. We lobbed a few jokes back and forth to one another, mostly having to do with the seemingly angry voice we kept hearing a few minutes before, but at this point we did not seem to be getting any obvious responses.

"Were you a mortician?" I asked. A quick reply came from the same voice we had heard several minutes before.

"NO! Fuck you!" Again, the vulgarity this voice used was an indicator of the anger and frustration of whatever

energy was coming through, but we kept pressing. I did not want to let this thing off the hook while we were getting immediate and intelligent responses, so we kept trying anything we could think to get it to respond.

"Turn the flashlight on," Courtney asked pleasantly.

"You do it, BITCH," was the quick response she got following her request.

At that point, the responses seemed to dwindle, but this having gone on for over ten minutes was outrageous. All three of us were really taken aback. Standing in a room that has no air movement and echoes constantly, the Ghost Box takes its toll on someone's ears eventually, so we turned it off to see if we could hear anything or feel anything outside of what had just happened. We continued our interrogation and both Courtney and I felt something tug on our pants at almost the exact same time, and I noted that as it happened, all the lights on the K-II came on very strong.

"I just felt something touch my leg," I said calmly.

"Let's go." [EVP] A whispering voice came over the recorder as if it is right next to me.

"I did too! Just now, it was like something grabbed at my pants leg," Courtney apparently felt the same thing I did right around the same time.

"Let go!" [EVP] Another whispery voice came clearly through the recorder as Courtney and I tried to figure out what seemed to be grabbing at us.

"What the hell?! I swear, I just saw a shadow go from one side of the doorway to the other outside!" I told Courtney and Jared.

Neither of them had seen what I had just seen, but it was reason enough to leave this room behind and head back out so we could try to see what everyone else was doing upstairs.

"Demon." [EVP] Yet another whispery voice came over my recorder just before I shut down this particular recording session.

We headed upstairs to check on everyone else and things seemed to be fairly quiet, as everyone was starting to wind down for the evening. Russ and I went through the house with Shane, including the basement, and nothing really seemed to be out of the ordinary, so we were about to start packing up. It had been a long and eventful evening. Courtney and I decided to make one last trip downstairs.

We began our final interrogation of the night, and Courtney and I were quite condescending and were daring whatever had grabbed both of us earlier to come back out and give us something significant that we could end the evening on. We were set up behind the cement wall in the back of the basement and were pretty vulgar and arrogant with our provocations. Suddenly the air seemed to change as we were both getting a pretty good chuckle out of our smartass mouths.

"Whoa, dude! I just felt like cobwebs were draped over my head. Is there anything on me?" Courtney asked as she turned to let me to see if anything was on her. There was not.

"No, I don't see anything, do you feel that? It suddenly got really cold here," I stated, and she agreed as I grabbed the Mel-Meter to confirm my feelings. Sure enough, the temperature quickly dropped from a baseline of about 74 degrees and quickly dropped to 61; 60; 59.

"Holy shit!" Courtney jumped a little as we watched the temperature fluctuations on the Mel-Meter.

"What's wrong?" I asked.

"Something just picked up my crystal and dropped it; like this," she told me as she demonstrated the crystal pendant around her neck having been picked up so it was sticking straight out and then dropped back down to its original position.

"I'll get you." [EVP] A disturbing voice was picked up clearly as though someone or something was standing right between us.

"That's crazy. What are you trying to tell us???" I asked loudly, hoping we would get something big to happen just one more time before we leave for the night.

"You're mine." [EVP] The same eerie voice came through clearly one more time.

After a few more minutes, things seemed to have calmed down, so we decided to wrap things up and began packing up all the equipment. Between the five of us, we were able to get all the cameras taken down and the cable packed up rather quickly. We said our goodbyes to Shane and his girlfriend as they took off for the night. He had just asked me to lock up once we were finished.

We said goodbye to Russ, Julie, and Courtney as they pulled out once we had locked up the house. They thanked us for having them up. I was just glad it seemed to be worth the long drive they made to come and investigate with us. My initial feelings I had about Russ were spot on. What a great group of people. I was very lucky to have come in contact with them and get a chance to work with such good folks. Jared and I put the finishing touches on everything and locked up the house. We got in the car and hit the road.

"Damn, dude, I'm wiped," Jared said just a few minutes after we hit the road.

"I hear you there bro, that place is totally crazy."

After a few more minutes, I had convinced Jared to get some rest and let him know I would be fine to stay awake. He was out like a light within a couple minutes. It would be a long drive home, but I believed the night had been well worth it.

After a little longer on the road, Jared was out cold and I could not get rid of the feeling that was overwhelming me that something was off. For some reason, I kept feeling like every time I looked in the rearview mirror I should expect to see something, or someone. It was creepy and a feeling that I could not shake. I felt like the air in the car was much heavier than even the other previous times that I had felt something similar. I just felt like something was out of place or wrong, a threatening type of feeling. We left Shane's house behind us and although I could not put my finger on what it was, I knew something was wrong. Only time would tell what it was, but I was sure something would happen.

We made it back safely, after narrowly avoiding a large deer that had seemed to try to commit suicide by running head on into my car while I was driving seventy-five miles an hour. That got my heart beating and Jared had been shaken awake by the breaks and car swerving to miss by a couple feet certain disaster. What a jacked-up night this had been. I finally got Jared to his house and made it home. I decided to wait until the next day to load all the data to my computer and start going through it. This night simply felt like it needed to end and the sun would be coming up within a couple hours.

Fifteen

THE FOLLOWING

When we arrived back from the investigation, exhaustion settled over me like it never had in my life. For many years I had been used to working very long and stressful hours but even looking back over my days in the military, I could not recall another time that I felt so completely drained and utterly unconscious on my feet. The first thing I typically do when I arrive at home following an investigation is cleanse my protective stones with incense, and on this very early morning, I was too tired to complete this process. This ritual theoretically releases any energy from the stones that may have attempted to attach itself to me. I had been told, the incense cleansing safely releases all energy and allows me to be protected from anything that may wish to do me harm. This process has worked perfectly for me since I began doing it over the course of my investigative career. I figured I would get to it after sleeping for a little while, and was out before my head even hit the pillow. My consistently reliable process was never completed.

The alarm went off way too early on this Monday morning following the latest investigation at Shane's house. I had not felt right since we arrived back home and something was just out of place. I was very edgy and was just hoping I was overly exhausted.

"Brandon, Hey! Hehehe," an eerie female-sounding voice came from the darkest corner of my room as I quickly snapped out of the fog of just waking up. I was immediately covered from head to toe with chills. As I looked into the corner where the voice had come from, it went from blacker than black to a slightly lighter shade of darkness. Of course, seeing something like this could be attributed to having just woken up and being extremely tired from an eventful weekend. I saw what I saw and felt like there was an obvious change in the darkness of the corner. I popped out of bed and decided it was best to go ahead and move on with my morning, so I proceeded to take a shower and get ready for work. Nothing else seemed to happen, but for the remainder of the day I felt like I was being watched. This feeling had become somewhat normal over the last several weeks, but today just felt a little different.

My suspicions were confirmed as I went to say hello to Jason when I got to work, and he looked at me with a look I had never seen. I have seen him when he looks concerned and can read his body language very well, but when he looked at me this time, it seemed like I made him uncomfortable. I was approaching him to give him a rundown of the investigation like I always did when he couldn't make the trip.

Our entire conversation was uncomfortable.

"What is the matter with you, buddy?" I asked him in an almost irritated tone.

"Nothing, we should have lunch and talk," he told me, and I agreed.

We went to lunch that day, which turned more into a meeting trying to plan out what we would do with Shane's house. It was time to start developing the plan to make a positive difference in the house. All through the process we had been discussing different options and things we thought may be going on, so at this point we felt comfortable with what was in front of us. Jason had mentioned that I needed to keep my head on a swivel because something was wrong. He could not put his finger on exactly what was happening, but it made him uncomfortable and worried for my safety.

"I don't know exactly what is there, but I feel like it was invited in and would be next to impossible to remove." Jason told me in a serious tone.

"If it is that difficult to remove, what am I supposed to tell the family?"

"I don't know, but I feel like nobody should live in that house—ever. There is a very small chance that we could do something, but chances are, we would need the person that opened the door to be present in closing it. We both know that won't happen," Jason continued.

"Well shit. Do you feel like whatever this thing is can follow us?" I asked.

"Oh yes, it can do whatever it wants. I feel like it was called in, and when it was, there was an opening that will be nearly impossible to close, especially without the person that opened it. The dungeon room feels like a portal to me. It is basically a highway for anything evil that may want to cross over and interact in any way with people. I think that is why people have such a tendency to be so depressed and short while they are in the house. I hesitate to ever go back there, although you know I will in order to keep trying to find answers, but I have never seen anything like this in a private home." Jason is attempting to explain the dangers of this house.

"Alright, so at this point I need to let the family know that it is our recommendation that they board the place up and never return? That seems insane to me. How the hell can something like this take over an entire house?!" I was flustered with the conversation, but in my heart, I felt like Jason was right.

"Yeah, it is rare to see things get such a strong grip on a home, but I believe completely that something very powerful has been called in and there is little to nothing any of us can do about it. They even pointed out that during the cleansing when they invited in the preacher that the place reacted violently. I don't feel like there is anything we can do without having the person responsible for inviting in the energy," Jason continued.

"So I take it our feeling about there being some type of inhuman energy is correct?" I asked.

"Yes, there is a demon in the home and it can easily bring in other demons as well. That is why it is so confrontational. It doesn't cower to our threats or commands. It obviously wants every person in the house to know that it is there and that it will do whatever it needs to do to make sure it is left alone. I think I picked up a name, but I'm not positive, and I'm not comfortable saying it." Jason explained as best he could, knowing I would not like what he was telling me.

"Okay. I need to talk to Shane and his family." Our conversation came to an end and I felt like banging my head into a brick wall. I was having a difficult time accepting the fact that there was nothing we can do about what was going on. I trusted him though.

As things tend to work out on occasion, I arrived back at work to discover an email from Shane. It explained that he and his mother had decided to move him out of the house that day. The family wanted nothing to do with the house anymore and I really could not blame them. He had mentioned that an old man had offered to purchase the house from the family and they were going to sell it to him. The reality that this case would remain open forever was almost too much to comprehend. The only comfort I had was the fact that we were not leaving the case open by choice. Shane had given me a method to contact the old man, but there was never a response when I attempted to reach out. Of course I never let him know exactly who I was or what my business was with the house. I was fearful for this man because I kept hearing over and over what Jason had told me.

"Nobody should live in that house—ever."

I did not want to frighten the man but had planned on discussing all we had experienced there on our previous trips, but I never had the opportunity because he did not respond. This case would haunt me in many ways, maybe for the rest of my life. I knew that without a doubt. It had given me a new perspective, but I knew I needed to take the lessons learned from this case and understand that these things happen and we have no control over them. The bottom line was Shane felt safe and happy when he was not in the house, so for his long-term health and happiness, I knew they were making the right decision.

The highway of demonic activity was destined to remain open for eternity. I knew even if the house was torn down or even burned down, chances were the portal would remain open. This was the first time I really understood firsthand that there is a reason for so much evil in the world. In short, it finds its way into the world and sometimes it cannot be stopped. The most frightening thing about this to me is the fact that despite our desire to fight the good fight and our faith in God's presence and strength, the battle between good and evil has been going on since the beginning of time and would continue until the end of it. All we can do is learn our lessons and prepare for the inevitability of facing these dark forces again in our future.

That night I had a difficult time winding down and getting to the point where I felt I could get a decent amount of rest. I could not get this case off my mind—I kept replaying everything in my head. How many times within the last few weeks I had been reminded that I had immersed myself in something I didn't entirely understand. I knew it happened for a reason, so I eventually was able to close my eyes.

5:12 AM

I can't breathe! Ahhh! I can't move!!! Umph; Umph; my breath is taken from my body and the pain is unbearable. Repeatedly; I am being beaten. There is a roaring growl and an evil laughter surrounding me … I … can't … breathe … somebody help me!!!

5:13 AM

I open my eyes as I lay on my stomach in excruciating pain. The roaring growls continue; I can only stare at the clock as the minutes feel like hours. I am surrounded by evil and the pain gets worse and worse. This evil laughter continues; umph; I am being clubbed up and down my back. I am paralyzed with pain and fear, "I just need to look at the foot of my bed!" my mind keeps repeating as every attempt I make to move is snuffed out as the assault continues.

5:14 AM

"No ... no ... NOOOOOOO!!!" I am being rabidly assaulted; the pain is completely unbearable and I can't make a sound; all I want to do is scream out for help but I can't. Umph; another club across my back as there is piercing pain as I am being raped; the growling and snarling; and menacing laughter continues.

5:15 AM

"Please; I beg you; umph; please; stop!!!! Make it stop, please God; help me!" My mind is begging for a reprieve but the beating and assault continues violently. The lower half of my body is screaming in pain but I still cannot move a muscle. I am going to die here in my bed.

5:16 AM

The minutes tick by like hours; the assault continues; I try with every fiber of my being to simply roll over, as I had to defend myself.

"Fuck; fucker; motherfucker! DIE!!!" the all too familiar inhuman and evil voice growls from the foot of my bed as I lay there helpless; the assault continues; this is no dream. The tears of pain roll from my eyes and I still cannot breathe; I cannot move; I am going to die; Umph, the beating continues.

5:17 AM

I can't take it, please, I'm sorry; God help me! My mind cannot comprehend what is going on; this is no dream. Wait.

My leg begins to come to life as the growling and snarling continues; one final club to my kidney, my breath is gone. I am covered with cold sweat and begin to shiver as the deep, aching pain begins to throb.

I throw my body over with all my might as the laughter ceases; I see the blackness disappear into the wall as I lay on my still-crippled right side. I am completely panicked and am slowly regaining the use of my limbs. I lay there, crying like a baby; "Why???" I knew the answer as my mind asked the question. The pain was still unbearable.

5:18 AM

I am lying on my back in shock. I still cannot find it in me to breathe regularly. My body was in so much pain and I knew what had just happened. I had just reaped what I had sown. My mocking and daring of this dark force to do something finally kicked in, and it decided it was time to do something. I had been raped and beaten by a force that was not human. I knew I had broken ribs and was bleeding from the assault; I lay there helpless in my bed covered in cold sweat and knew I was the victim of an attack by a force so evil there would be no remorse, there would be no apology. I knew life would never be the same. Shame came over me in waves as I lay there. Crippled with fear and pain, I could do nothing. Any energy I had in my body had been ripped from me and I lay there simply staring into the darkness of my room and did not know what to do. I did not know who could help me, and I knew exactly what had happened and why. This was my doing. I asked for it, yet, nobody deserves it.

I reached up and turned my clock off as the clock strikes 5:21 a.m. I could not watch the minutes tick by any longer. I was broken emotionally and physically and felt like I would never be able to get out of my bed again. I wondered why it didn't just kill me. Maybe leaving someone in their own pain and shame is a worse punishment; maybe this had been yet another warning. Maybe whatever this force was knew I would never be back to Shane's house, so it took the opportunity to leave its mark permanently written on my body and face.

After another hour of lying there speechless and powerless, I decided I needed to know what my body looked like. I could feel the bruising setting in and could feel the blood trickling out of me. I was in shock. I slowly made my way to the bathroom as I could barely walk and could not stand up straight. I felt like I had just been beaten with some sort of club. I was shocked to find there was no bruising around my kidneys and ribs, where the pain was still as sharp as it had been during the attack. No evidence of the assault. I sat down to check myself for bleeding; it was almost too painful to check, but I did, and I was bleeding. I cannot put into words the embarrassment and shame that had overcome me. I had been assaulted by something I underestimated. The one-time safe haven of my home, my room, had been tarnished and broken into by something that leaves no fingerprints. Whatever it was, it left no sign of it having been here. But it left scars all over my body, mind, and soul.

The pain lasted for days. I was barely able to get out of bed for several days following the attack. I was able to get in touch with Jason and had begged him to come over because I was scared to death that this thing might return. He gladly came over to the house during his lunch break the very next day, having heard the desperation in my voice.

"Whoa, are you alright?!" he asked as I greeted him.

"No, something happened; I can't," I tried to tell him the details but couldn't bring myself to do it.

"Dude, there was some type of demon here, are you okay? I feel like the energy is dissipated though," Jason said, trying to comfort me. I knew what he knew and we were both very shaken.

The words incubus and succubus were discussed as Jason and I sat calmly and knew something had come to make sure we would never return to that house. Shane had reported being held down in his bed on several occasions, but this went much further than that. I had been crippled and assaulted for several minutes while being completely awake. I could not even wrap my mind around this being possible, but I had the pain to prove it was very possible. Not only possible—it had actually happened. My only hope was that whatever this demon was, it had made its point and would never return. Jason and I immediately went through the process of cleansing the area as we were alone in the house. We wanted to make sure we kept this energy at bay. We burned sage and I thoroughly cleansed my stones with incense. We could not allow this creature to overcome this house as it had the other.

Several more days went by, and slowly the darkness seemed to continue to dissipate to the point where I had become more functional. I was unable to find it in me to tell my brother or anyone else this. I had told Jason about the entire thing, and he made me feel better stating that he would be surprised if it came back. Over the course of several days after we had cleansed the house, I found it easier to sleep with each passing night after I had lain awake for almost forty-eight hours following the attack. The pain was nearly gone after about a week, but the damage had been done. I knew I would never be able to shake this, and I had to seriously consider whether or not what I was doing was worth it.

Whatever we had been dealing with obviously had the ability to find me no matter where I was. If it could find me, it could most certainly find anyone else that may have accompanied me, so my newest fear was that this thing would put someone else through the misery I had experienced. I had a lot of soul searching to do and did not know if I would be able to overcome what had happened. The overwhelming realization that I brought this upon myself was almost too much to bear. I think the worst part was the fact that I did not know how to avoid something like this in the future. Since the day I had begun investigating, I had not been mentally prepared for the possible repercussions. I had prepared myself to deal with dreams and even strange little occurrences in everyday life, but I had not been prepared to deal with such a vicious and very real attack—it is impossible to prepare yourself for this type of event. That night had changed my life on just about every level, and I needed to search deep within my soul to figure out whether or not I was broken. I needed to make a decision as to whether or not I had it in me to keep doing what I had felt for so long I was called to do. My greatest fear to this point was something like this happening to someone I was with. If this happened to my brother, his wife, Jason, Jared, or anyone else who had accompanied me to that dark highway of evil, I didn't know if I could live with myself. Of course, everyone that involved themselves with these investigations had to accept a certain level of responsibility and understand the inherent risks.

I knew I would have to tell everyone about what had happened. They needed to know what was possible so they could make an intelligent and informed decision about continuing with their involvement. First, I needed to figure out where I stood. It would take time and I was determined to make a good decision. I would pray and I would ask every question I could think to ask. Am I truly willing to put myself at risk for these types of assaults? Is this worth it? I believed with all my heart that we all have the ability to save lost souls and to help people in desperate need who live with these dark forces every single day. I needed to take all of this into account as I made my decision. The one comforting thing in my mind was the fact that I knew without a doubt that I would be taken in the direction I needed to go. My faith had not been shaken. I knew I was being tested and I would keep a level head and understand that sometimes the greatest tests lead to the greatest path.

Sixteen

ANOTHER DAY

As I awake to another day, I have a feeling in my gut. Something has changed. It has been weeks since I had to put a permanent stamp of "OPEN" next to the status of the case at Shane's former home. As the days went by and life moved on, I had been unable to put it behind me and was not quite ready to accept the fact that this would be a case that would haunt me forever.

I still keep in touch with Shane from time to time just to see how he is doing. He moved out of the house and the family was finally able to sell the home after months of trying. It is my understanding none of them have been back. Shane told me he has had no problems whatsoever since he moved out and is much happier and feels safe in his new home.

We never had an opportunity to try to rid the home of whatever was there. If in fact there was the soul of Emily or any other person that might be stuck in that house, we would never have a chance to help them rest peacefully. I knew the living people that had been involved in this case would be fine, the fact that we were unable to help any poor souls that may be lost in the depths of darkness that had taken hold of the house will bother me on a very deep level for the rest of my life. Jason had been convinced this was simply a situation that could not be repaired. I was unable to contact the new owner of the house, and Shane and his family simply wanted to put the place behind them. I could not blame them. The bottom line was they felt much better with the current situation. Shane had not slept in fear for months. That is about all I could ask for, a calming of the lives for those people that had lived in terror for so long.

The progress being made in my daily life and in my mind was slow, but it allowed me to function more and more normally as the days went by. The dark cloud that had loomed over my head was dissipating slowly, but I could feel a difference in the air around me. I had since gone back to Haun's Mill a couple times because it was a place that seemed to bring me peace and a calming feeling. As horrific as the events were that had taken place there so many years ago, I could not help but feel a serene feeling to the place before the sun went down. As soon as the sun disappeared behind the Missouri hills, the place took on a whole different personality. During my latest visit, I had something come over me that gave me confidence that I knew which path to take.

For years I have felt that I have been called to this work. Most people cannot understand this calling. They cannot understand why I do what I do. I actively seek out darkness and evil with the hope that I can help people find peace in their lives. I put myself at risk and determined that I would find ways to do what I am so passionate about while minimizing the risk to those around me. The strength and passion of those I work with helps me drive on. We ultimately just want to help those in need and attempt to help lost souls find their peaceful eternal rest. And I would travel and research different aspects of the world and figure out a ways to continue to do so.

One day, I simply woke up and felt the strength within me to look past my recent nightmare and clearly see the path before me. I knew I had the strength and protection of God, despite not having any active support from the "Holy" organizations. There is an unspoken rule among most organized religions that seems to want to avoid the discussion of the existence of evil in the world. Sure, there is discussion in the organized Masses they perform for their congregations, but when it came to actively seeking out and destroying the darkness that ruins lives and souls, they quickly go silent and hide behind the rule that in order to involve yourself with these things, you must be an official "man of the cloth," or they say you do not have the ability to help these people. That being said, these "Men of the Cloth" make little effort to seek out those needing assistance. I knew my calling required me to learn and know as much as I could retain about how to find and rid the world of such evils. I may only play a small part, but in my eyes, I am called to help others and ask nothing in return. I want to educate those wishing to learn about these dark forces and I want to know as much as I can know about how all the different cultures would go through the process of cleansing homes and lands that are infested with such evil.

Not only would I continue to pursue my passion, but I was reinvigorated knowing that I was stronger than ever. My eyes were wide open and I could now wrap my head around things that had previously been almost mythical in my mind. We are taught from an early age that the Boogie Man does not exist, and there is nothing hiding in our closet waiting to come out and torment us while we lie in bed. I do not dispute the need to comfort our children, but there is a fine line between protecting them and grooming them to go through their lives with their eyes closed to reality. I refer often to my childhood and the teachings of the Church throughout my life. I was thankful to be able to, at this point in my life, see the world from a perspective that allows for both common sense and spirituality. I felt I was becoming one with my surroundings and would never again underestimate the strength of the world.

Many different paranormal teams find a new place to investigate every weekend, which makes them investigators, but I also see them as thrill seekers. Thrill seekers will very rarely make a positive difference in our field's progress. They may stumble across an amazing piece of "evidence" and post it for the world to see all over a website, but they will never pursue answers as to why something is going on where it is going on. I do not intend to come across as arrogant; I am simply trying to paint the picture of how my thought process has morphed since experiencing something I never thought possible. I was able to look more clearly at the big picture instead of allowing myself to go about this process with a shortsighted point of view that would never lend itself to helping others and educating those wishing to learn.

I was able to establish what was becoming in my eyes a sure-fire way to anticipate where I needed to look in order to find active locations. I spent the next few weeks developing a plan that would allow me to simply point to a location on a map and know without a doubt that it was a place of interest that would be very likely to be the home to unexplained activity on a grand scale. Of course I always say, if you believe these things exist, then thinking they only exist in cemeteries or old prisons or hospitals is very naive. Yes, these types of places often have activity for obvious reasons, but why not pursue a scientific method to anticipate paranormal activity? So often it seems we point to a battlefield and state, "That place is haunted;

there was a bloody battle that took place years ago." Well, why not ask the question, "Is there a reason the battle took place there? Had there ever been a battle near that location prior to this particular battle?" In short, we forget constantly that the lands we inhabit today have existed since the beginning of time. I cannot tell you how often I have heard people wishing they could go investigate the paranormal in Europe because everything is so old. Well, in my mind, I am simply thinking these people seem to think the land we are standing on just happened to pop up when the United States was established. The truth is, countless tribes existed on these lands for thousands of years before we did. They fought with each other and practiced their own rituals. There has been history written on these lands longer than we have known the land exists.

For this reason, I have been determined to figure out how to find locations that contain certain energies. These energies have been followed for thousands of years and are very often the sites of tribal burial grounds, cursed lands, or the sites of even bloodier and more brutal battles than our history books may ever know. Very often, when you dig deep enough, these places are some of the most active places you will ever find. I continued to develop this theory and went to many nearby locations that my method pointed me to and have yet to be disappointed.

The nightmares were still there, although they became less common as the nights went by. My Nemesis was always there whether he was nearby or hiding in the shadows. He was always accompanied by the other man, the man who had shown up alongside the Nemesis so many years ago. They were always there. The overwhelming feeling of being stalked had subsided for the time being. I felt as though whatever attacked me after investigating Shane's house had made its point, although I now had a very clear understanding that these evil beings work on their own time frame. They do not know or care about the concept of time. They have eternity to do their horrific work and they can attack as they please. There is always a worry in the back of my mind that something bigger may happen at some point. I believe evil exists and is extraordinarily powerful. Look around and ask yourself what would be the most effective way to destroy the human spirit. These beings have a psychological advantage—the ability to instill depression and fear into the hearts of the living always exists. The easiest way to hurt someone is to slowly chip away at their psyche and make them fear the world around them. Force people to wonder whether the God they pray to truly exists, instill doubt in their minds.

Yes, evil is ever-present and looking for any opportunity to ravage the spirit of any person that may be vulnerable. We are all inherently vulnerable, so we are all potential targets for the Ruiner of Souls and his minions. My intention is to teach people in need that their faith should never waver and they should allow the love in their hearts to shine through and spill over into the lives of people around them. The best way to combat this deception and torment is to forgive and to love. Always keep the faith and understand that the existence of evil is proof enough of the existence of a greater good. Pursuing these stories and locations is just one way I feel able to find true progress in this field of research.

I have been called crazy, unstable, obsessed, and everything in between. I simply allow anyone their opinion and hope they do not experience the horrors I have seen. The phrase "ignorance is bliss" comes to mind. I simply include them in my prayers and hope they never have to experience the cold reality of what true evil exists in the world. My goals do not include converting nonbelievers to believers. I am of the opinion that people are welcome to believe whatever they wish, and I hope they live a long and happy life. I have accepted my calling and will travel to the ends of the Earth if necessary to help those in need and seek the answers I need to questions that have been asked since the beginning of time. This does not make me special, it simply makes me aware. This is how I have chosen to live my life and my only hope is in the end, I am able to help as many people as I can in living a happy and true life without dealing with constant fear. I hope to be able to allow lost or imprisoned souls to rest in eternal peace.

I had developed a plan and felt like it was very possible to put it into action, and it would allow me to tell these incredible stories. My lifelong passions of independent film and writing would come into play as these are two very clear methods I would develop in order to tell the stories of forgotten history and the lives of those that deal with things most people only experience in a movie theater. These are stories that write themselves over the course of time; I simply want to carry the pen and point the camera in the right direction.

I have been blessed with amazing people to work with and could tell they were beginning to understand the bigger picture. It is very easy to shoot for and hope for some type of immediate notoriety for doing the work we do, the majority of the people out there that conduct investigations have a goal in mind of finding themselves on a television series or something to that effect. These things do not appeal to me because I believe the bigger picture and larger goal is to simply help people and educate people. Doing this requires time and patience. Developing a true case study of a location provides the opportunity to touch people's lives and hopefully bring peace to a location that has long needed it.

This old Victorian house will haunt my thoughts for the remainder of my days, of that I am very sure. There are very few days that pass without me wondering what would have ultimately happened if we were given the opportunity to truly confront this evil force. I will never know, and understanding that I will never know is what is so unsettling. Shane and his family have moved on, yet I have such difficulty letting go. I have no doubt that whatever took over that house and followed me, before changing my life forever, will meet again someday. My endless pursuit of answers will continue. Each passing investigation leaves a mark on my soul. I will bear these scars for eternity and continue to fight for the souls of the departed and those out there that are forced to live their lives in fear of the unknown. I will not stop. With my faith in a greater good and love on my side, I will face my fears as I seek the truth.

MY TERRIFYING CLASH WITH A DEMONIC ENTITY

ENCOUNTER
with
HELL

ALEXIS McQUILLAN

Encounter with Hell
My Terrifying Clash with a Demonic Entity
Alexis McQuillan

The events in this story are true, but the names and locations have been changed to protect the reader. Alexis is a psychic who never believed in demons until she came face to face with pure evil. This is her true story of battling a terrifying entity that was so powerful it turned her life upside down and put her in mortal danger…

Her nightmare begins shortly after she and her husband relocate to a small lakeside community. After hearing rumors about the nearby Matthews residence, Alexis investigates the nineteenth-century house and its spirit inhabitants. She soon finds herself caught in a demon's snare of violent fury—subjecting her to deep growls, a malevolent force attacking her in bed, and phantom apparitions, ultimately leading to a horrific spiritual battle with a demon hell-bent on her destruction.

978-0-7387-3350-0, 5³⁄₁₆ x 8, 216 pp.   **$14.99**